WHEN'S RECESS?
PLAYING YOUR WAY THROUGH THE STRESSES OF LIFE

Howard Papush

TRAFFORD

Canada • UK • Ireland • USA • Spain

© Copyright 2004, Howard Papush.
All rights reserved.

No part of this publication may be reproduced, stored in a retrieval system, or transmitted, in any form or by any means, electronic, mechanical, photocopying, recording, or otherwise, without the written prior permission of the author.

Note for Librarians: a cataloguing record for this book that includes Dewey Decimal Classification and US Library of Congress numbers is available from the National Library of Canada. The complete cataloguing record can be obtained from the National Library's online database at:
www.nlc-bnc.ca/amicus/index-e.html
ISBN 1-4120-3346-2

TRAFFORD

Offices in Canada, USA, Ireland, UK and Spain
This book was published *on-demand* in cooperation with Trafford Publishing. On-demand publishing is a unique process and service of making a book available for retail sale to the public taking advantage of on-demand manufacturing and Internet marketing. On-demand publishing includes promotions, retail sales, manufacturing, order fulfilment, accounting and collecting royalties on behalf of the author.

Book sales in Europe:
Trafford Publishing (UK) Ltd., Enterprise House, Wistaston Road Business Centre, Wistaston Road, Crewe CW2 7RP UNITED KINGDOM
phone 01270 251 396 (local rate 0845 230 9601)
facsimile 01270 254 983; info.uk@trafford.com

Book sales for North America and international:
Trafford Publishing, 6E–2333 Government St.,
Victoria, BC V8T 4P4 CANADA
phone 250 383 6864 (toll-free 1 888 232 4444)
fax 250 383 6804; email to bookstore@trafford.com

www.trafford.com/robots/04-1173.html

10 9 8 7 6 5 4 3

TO MY FIRST PLAYMATE,

MY MOM

and

TO MY FAVORITE PLAYMATE,

TIMOTHY MASON

ACKNOWLEDGEMENTS

How many of you have ever watched the Academy Awards® and groaned when a winner exclaimed he had a long list of people he needed to thank for their support? And then droned on and on as the music started to play, warning him to stop! How boring I used to think. But ironically I am now in that same position.

There are so many people I wish to acknowledge for helping make this book a reality. Hopefully the music won't start playing before I finish! You, reader, have the right to turn the page at any time. However, if you are a member of my family, or one of my close friends, or a key business associate who gave me a start with your company, you might want to hang on for a bit.

The first person I wish to acknowledge is Adryan Russ, my dear friend and editor. Besides encouraging me to write this book in the first place, she was from day one a trusted advisor, critic, and suporter. She deserves special praise.

The Papush family has always loved and supported me. Thanks Joel, Cindy, Gregg, Michele, Gary, Sharie, Lee, Andrew, Gene, Michael, Aunt Sarah, Aunt Harriett and Cousin Bob Becker for being there.

To all those great friends who rooted me on during this long incubation period I am eternally grateful. Some are authors in their own right: individuals such as Raysa Bonow, Wayne Dyer, Mary Dawn Gladson, Laurie Grand, Marilyn Hamel, Jane Heller, Brad Lemack, and Ross Shafer. You are all strong role models for me.

Extra thanks go to Ross for pushing and pushing until I got this book done, to Ted Cordes for doing such meticulous proof-reading, and to the talented Rick Stockwell for his "scintillating" photograph of me on the back cover.

Next credit is due pals Barbara Dreyfuss, Bob Maurer, John Wingler, George Colman, and Gary Leo who believed in my cause so totally that they actually hired me.

Then there are all those close friends who came into my life and stayed to cheer me on. In order of appearance they include: Penny Barthold, Sydney Lapidus, Mark Grand, Steve Cooperstein, Bernie & Vicki Teeman, Doug Barton, Richard Caine, Neil Koenigsberg, Bill & Barbara Farlie, Terry Hart, B.J. Markel, Bill Lustig, Christopher Harner, Marianne Harner, Perry King, Larry Weiss, Steve Dacri, Rigo Banuelos, Bill Derby, Dale Cooke, Dick Neu, Brian Miller, Lloyd Kajikawa, Patrick Olesko, Kathleen Caine, Robert Butler, Chuck Silver, Elliott Kristal, Lynn Lustig, Robert Curtis, Jim Petzke, Noah Markel, Mark Saucedo, Michael Forrester, Steve & Karen Kohn, Ira Denmark, Al & Keli Prado, and Vivian & Charlie Taylor. Thanks for all your support.

It is a pleasure to acknowledge several professional associates who saw the value of my "play" concepts right away. Glenda Berman, Rhoda Cahan, Andrea Edwards, Jim Giraldin, Babette Heimbuch, Steve Leder, Steve Mathis, Bonnie Nash, Fred Nichols, and Sylvia Woodside were among the first to introduce LET'S PLAY AGAIN programs to their organizations, and continue to believe in my cause.

Thanks also to journalist Daniel Foster, who interviewed me numerous times for his stories in leading magazines and newspapers, which first brought me to the attention of the general public.

There are five other people who deserve special recognition. Though they are now departed, I think of them often and know they are watching over me and proud of my accomplishments. Thank you Dad, and pals Bruce Fox, Dick Howard, George Miller and Vernon Wheat. I miss you.

TABLE OF CONTENTS

PROLOGUE 9
INTRODUCTION 13

PART ONE – LET'S PLAY AGAIN
1   ARE YOU HAVING FUN YET? 21
2   TAKING TIME TO CELEBRATE "BEING ALIVE" 25
3   THE MOST CREATIVE PEOPLE ARE PLAYFUL 28
4   CLOSE YOUR EYES AND LET'S TAKE A TRIP 31
5   CHILDHOOD NEVER LETS GO OF US 34
6   DR. PLAY'S FAVORITE GAMES 36
7   JUST CALL ME "TEX," AND WHAT DO I CALL YOU? 43
8   BLUE GLASSES' REBELLION AND OTHER STRANGE TALES 47
9   THE DAY OF THE IGUANA 51
10 RECESSING RECESS 55

PART TWO – "PETER PAN" BEGINS TO FLY
11 PLAY—THE EARLY YEARS 61
12 PARDON ME BUT AREN'T YOU…? 65
13 WHO'S AFRAID OF BIG, BAD BILL? 68
14 THE JOYS OF STICKBALL 71
15 ONE "PENNY" THAT'S WORTH A FORTUNE 74

PART THREE – IS THIS TV OR AM I IN A SANDBOX?
16 SUPER GUIDE CONDUCTS THE NBC TOUR 81
17 A CANDID LOOK AT "CANDID CAMERA" 85
18 WELCOME TO THE FUN HOUSE 90
19 JOHNNY CARSON LIKES TO PLAY 95
20 DON'T BE NERVOUS—YOU'RE GREGORY PECK! 99
21 "SAY HEY" WILLIE MAYS 102
22 ZERO MOSTEL "FIDDLES" AROUND 105
23 THE EVER PLAYFUL MEL BROOKS 108

PART FOUR – FEELING YOUNG— SCALPEL NOT REQUIRED!
24 THE SEARCH FOR PERPETUAL YOUTH 115
25 IT'S TIME YOUR INNER CHILD AND I HAD A TALK 118
26 REMEMBER WHEN? 123
27 AND NOW A WORD FROM THE SPONSORS 128
28 HOW DO YOU SPELL "NEOTENOUS"? 132

PART FIVE – GO TO WORK AND PLAY
29 CREATING FUN IN THE WORKPLACE 139
30 MY TOY IS BIGGER THAN YOUR TOY 142
31 PLAYING WITH YOUR FOOD 147
32 SKIP, SKIP... SKIP TO THE LOO 150
33 THE "PRAISE" GAME 152
34 20 FUN GAMES FOR THE OFFICE 156

PART SIX – PLAYING ANYTIME, ANYWHERE
35 GROWN-UPS HAVING FUN 169
36 THE BEST SURPRISE BIRTHDAY PARTY YOU'LL EVER GIVE 173
37 AN INVITATION TO AN "ADULTS ONLY" PARTY 175
38 XMAS TREE XTRAVAGANZAS 178
39 FANTASY BASEBALL FOR FUN AND PROFIT 183
40 HOW MUCH DO YOU BID FOR THIS DESSERT? 186
41 52 WEEKS OF PLAY IDEAS 188

PART SEVEN – CELEBRITY CHILDHOODS
42 TOM HANKS WAS ONCE A KID TOO! 195
43 MARVIN HAMLISCH HAD A TRAIN SET 198
44 HIDING OUT WITH SUZANNE SOMERS 201
45 PLAYING BALL WITH ACTOR ED HARRIS 205
46 PERRY KING'S FAVORITE PLAYMATE 208

PART EIGHT – ENJOYING THE FUN LIFE
47 EVERYDAY PLEASURES 213
48 IT'S TIME FOR A LITTLE "INTERNAL JOGGING" 216
49 THE NEW TECHNOLOGY—A GAME YOU CAN MASTER 218
50 YES, PLAYMATES, THERE "IS" A SANTA CLAUS! 222
51 DR. PLAY'S "HEALTHFUL HINTS" 225
52 HAVING FUN ON THE JOURNEY 228

PROLOGUE

"You are led through your lifetime by the inner learning creature, the playful spiritual being that is your real self."
—Richard Bach, American Author (1936-present)

On a stormy night in late January of 1978, a mysterious and profound moment occurred at the NBC Studios in California that changed the direction of my life and career.

Less than five months before, I had been hired away from *The Tonight Show Starring Johnny Carson*, where I had worked the previous four years as a television executive. Westinghouse Broadcasting Company had decided that I and a colleague, Paul Block, were the perfect guys to create and produce the pilot for a new daytime television series.

Now we were about to see the results of our labor. We had cast a talented group of young performers who were going over their final scripts, hoping too that their budding careers might be forever changed if our collaborative efforts were successful that night. Over the preceding months we had worked diligently to design a test show that would be entertaining and informational.

Our most important need was to ensure that the virtually unknown cast made an immediate impact and connection with the studio audience, and eventually with those decision-makers who would view the tape. For it was the station managers and the program directors who would ultimately decide whether this was the kind of program they wanted to buy and air on their stations.

Weeks before I had happened to mention this challenge to a fellow named David Smith, who was going to be a contributing personality on our series. Paul and I knew him from our *Tonight Show* days. He was an author/adventurer and frequent guest, who amused Johnny with his amazing escapades. During our conversation with David, he suggested that he referee a group-play activity for the pilot. He had in mind a game called "Yoga Tag," a two team event with lots of action and competition that eventually morphed into a cooperative effort. As he explained it to us, the game's surprise ending had all the players on the very same side. He thought it would be fun for both the audience and the participants.

Instinctively I felt that this was the perfect way to go. I had always known that when people are at play, they reveal an innocent, childlike side of themselves that is both fun and revealing for those who are watching. I could envision how this would be a unique way to show off the special personalities in "our family."

So on this very rainy night, back at our old stomping grounds at NBC, Paul and I watched the various segments being videotaped. Our wet, yet enthusiastic audience was enjoying each element. They were thrilled when celebrities Don Rickles, Chevy Chase, Marvin Hamlisch, George Carlin, and Doc Severinsen suddenly made surprise appearances in sketches.

Then we rolled out "Yoga Tag." As the game unfolded "our family" and two of our other celebrity guests—Suzanne Somers and LeVar Burton—found themselves romping and cavorting in a state of gleeful, unrehearsed play. How joyous they seemed! I checked out the audience too. It was amazing to see how involved they were, intently watching our performers fully involved in the energy of the game. No doubt they were enjoying what they were witnessing.

Suddenly a wave of deep feeling gripped me. Time seemed to stand still. I began to tremble as I heard a soft but insistent voice inside my head. At first I couldn't identify what it was saying. But soon the sound intensified and the words became specific and clear—

> "This is terrific! Wow, this is powerful!
> This play is so familiar! Remember
> what you're seeing. You've GOT to! It
> has a special meaning for your future!"

"It has meaning for my future?" I was puzzled. But my brain at the moment couldn't understand exactly what was going on. At a deep level, though, I knew I had been touched by something significant and that I needed to figure out what it meant.

Actually it took years before that veiled epiphany in the NBC Studios in Burbank more than 25 years ago finally became clear. By then I had created LET'S PLAY AGAIN, the transforming seminar that has given so many people hope that their jobs and their careers, and in fact their lives, can be less stressful, more creative, and so much more fun.

INTRODUCTION

"Choose a job you love and you will never have to work a day in your life."
—*Confucius, Chinese Philosopher (551-479 B.C.)*

When we were kids we got recess. Now that we're adults, we don't! This is an absolute fact and a recipe for disaster. Indeed not having the kind of "time out" we enjoyed as kids—the opportunity to drop everything and just play for the fun of it—is causing enormous issues for all of us as we deal with the challenges of the 21st Century.

Our work ethic is creating problems in the corporate world and getting in the way of our personal relationships. It's leading us into serious personal stress and a loss of the harmony and authentic communication we need with others in our lives. And it's robbing us of our joy.

A few years ago Bill Waterson, in his much beloved *Calvin & Hobbes* comic strip, highlighted the dilemma. In the particular episode, precocious Calvin, the 6-year-old who is usually depicted playing with his imaginary stuffed tiger pal Hobbes, is having a conversation with his father. He is trying to understand why his dad and other adults don't take recess. In the first panel of the strip he asks, "How come grownups don't go out to play?"

His father answers: "Grownups can only justify playing outside by calling it exercise, doing it when they'd rather not, and keeping records to quantify their performance."

Calvin thinks about that for a moment and then says, "That sounds like a job."

His father quickly answers, "Except you don't get paid."

In the final panel of the strip Calvin asks, "So play is worse than work?"

And his father replies, "Being a grownup is tough."

BEING A GROWNUP IS TOUGH

Calvin's dad is right—being a grownup is tough. Much is demanded of us. I bet you feel overworked and underpaid. You probably begin your day with a long commute, either sitting or standing on a crowded bus or train, or in your car surrounded by congested traffic and angry, out-of-control drivers. Your career may have become too demanding or utterly boring, and your boss probably expects even more of your time and energy. Lunch tasted lousy. You suspect the person whose desk is outside your office is plotting to get your job. You can't keep up with the E-mail or the faxes. And the vibrating pager or ringing cell phone attached to your hip is driving you crazy.

Waiting at home are bills that have to be paid, a lawn that needs to be mowed, and probably a mate who needs more of your time. Then there is a family to feed and aging parents to check up on. How do you find a way to deal with all of this?

Every day of our lives a voice deep within us tries to provide an answer. It asks over and over again, "When are we going to have some fun today? When are we going out to play?"

It's the voice of the child we once were, and it frequently makes this important request of us. It's a request that has the power to return us to our sanity. But do we listen? Or do we try to ignore the urgent appeal?

John Bradshaw, in his number one best-selling book, *Homecoming*, wrote extensively about how "we first see the world through the eyes of a little child and that inner child remains with us throughout our lives, no matter how outwardly 'grown up' and powerful we become."

So many adults unfortunately forget the value of their childhood days and the important lessons they learned through the act of playing.

- Play made us laugh and smile.
- Play eased our worry and tension.
- Play connected us to the others who were on the playground or in the sandbox.
- Play helped us to develop our imagination.
- Play provided energy.

- Play taught us to cope with difficult kids around us, and to learn whom to trust and whom not to trust.
- Play allowed us to take risks.
- Play gave us breathing room to solve our problems.

Lots of adults squelch that inner voice because they fear it will somehow do them harm. Somewhere in our development we were given the message from society that it was no longer OK to play, that we needed to grow up, that we had to be serious. Famed anthropologist Ashley Montagu scoffed at that, often calling adults "deteriorated children"!

One survey reported that children on average laugh and smile more than 200 times a day, while the typical adult laughs only seven times a day. Seven times a day! What happened? Why did we buy into the concept that seriousness is good and experiencing joy is bad?

It has been said that having fun through play is really taking time to "celebrate being alive." I believe that the celebrating should happen all during the day, wherever we are. It must not be monitored. If we feel we must stop reaching for this sense of joy, for example when we arrive at the job site, we are not only cheating ourselves but we're also cheating our employers.

For more than twelve years my LET'S PLAY AGAIN seminars have amused, surprised, delighted, refreshed, educated, and energized thousands of men and women across this country. I have brought a compelling idea to corporate executives, human resources directors, organizational development specialists, training managers, conference planners, social directors, ministers and rabbis, married couples, singles looking for a date, and anyone else who will listen. The message is that the act of recess—my form of "cooperative play"—brings laughter and peace to the hearts of people and helps to build morale, reduce stress, enhance creativity, and cement better understanding between individuals. The result is an interaction—in the workplace, the home, or the community—that provides more energy, harmony and productivity.

PLAY HELPS US TO ENDURE
This need for recess is manifest in all that we do. Being in touch

with our playful side, our silly side, the kid's voice that speaks to us all the time, helps us to endure. It has particular significance in our most important personal relationships.

Psychology Today magazine cited the research of Dr. Mark Knapp of the University of Texas and Dr. Phillip Glenn at Southern Illinois University, about the central role play has in the creation and support of intimacy. Their study showed that couples "often use highly personalized forms of play to enhance communication, strengthen bonds, and moderate conflict." As important, they observed, "the loss of playfulness in a marriage was strongly correlated with the onset of marital dysfunction." Not too long ago Dr. Joyce Brothers advised a husband who was spending too much time away from home that "the family that plays together stays together."

Perhaps those of you who are raising families will identify with the following scenario. You're busy doing one of those adult things, something you know is very necessary—preparing dinner, doing the laundry, washing the car—and one of your kids comes up to you and asks, "When are we going to do something fun?"

Or maybe it's the family dog, a ball planted securely between his teeth, looking at you with those sorrowful, yet hopeful eyes, which you know are saying, "Come on, let's play!"

If you're one of those people who keep putting your kid or the dog off, that never seems to have time to play with your children, or your spouse—I believe you're in serious trouble and this book is going to give you permission to change that.

PLAY HELPS US FEEL WELL

Important studies report that having a positive, happy attitude aids us when we're sick. Norman Cousins, who was editor of the *Saturday Review* for more than 30 years, wrote a best-selling book, *Anatomy of an Illness*, in which he detailed how he recovered from a painful and rare, degenerative disease of the connective tissues. With his doctor's permission, he took himself off his pain killers and instead used classic *Candid Camera* television shows and old Marx Brothers films to "belly laugh" his way back to health. In my "playshops" participants and I often find that the symptoms of bad colds and headaches magically disappear while we are in the midst of playing.

Dr. Carl Simonton, a cancer specialist and pioneer in holistic health, observes that playfulness is often one of the first things to disappear when people experience serious illness, and counsels that "play can be important for the patient and the family in getting back into the flow of life."

PLAY HAS THE POWER TO KEEP US YOUNG

With the "graying" of the Baby Boom Generation, many 40- and 50-year-olds have taken up a new cause—searching for the elusive Fountain of Youth. The media and the ads stress the need for working out at the gym and using cosmetic surgery to enhance that outer shell we present to the world on a daily basis. They imply that if we look in the mirror and see a more perfect nose, a collagen-enhanced face, or a chiseled body we are young once more.

But deep within our aging bodies will we really feel young? Will our hearts beat with the same sense of joy we exhibited when we were kids? The child within begs us to keep laughing and "jumping for joy." He appreciates every new thing he sees and touches. She asks questions about the world she lives in and she trusts people. His instinct is to reach out and to make new friends.

Those of us who are willing to embrace the things that the precious child is saying, and the messages it enthusiastically continues to share as the years pass, will never grow old! No matter what chronological age we reach, or the state of our bodies, when we as adults endeavor to retain these childlike qualities, we remain truly young. We have total access to our whimsy, our imagination, our sense of fun and adventure. There are easy ways for every single person to be in touch with the kid. It is my greatest wish to show you how.

JUST CALL ME "DR. PLAY"

Thousands of people now refer to me as "Dr. Play." I like that. I see myself like the friendly, neighborly doctor who once made house calls, found out what was ailing you, and then dispensed some prescriptive medicine to take care of the problem. Since I can't come to everyone's house, I want this book be a surrogate house call. Let me share with you how I got so smart about play, what happens in my seminars, and how incidences from my early life and my former television career prepared me to take on the role of Dr. Play. Let me show you ways that you can:

- Play with your families, your spouses, significant others, and your friends.
- Have fun when you're feeling stressed on the job, while you're stuck in traffic, or waiting in a checkout line at the market or the bank.
- Deal with those youngsters of yours who just don't want to listen.
- Use creative ideas, games, and toys to help you and your family's "celebration of being alive" become as fun-filled as perhaps it once was.

Come on—LET'S PLAY AGAIN!

PART ONE

LET'S PLAY AGAIN

CHAPTER 1

ARE YOU HAVING FUN YET?

> "Unless each day can be looked back upon by an individual as one in which he has had some fun, some joy, some real satisfaction, that day is a loss."
> —Dwight Eisenhower, 34th U.S. President (1890-1969)

Do you realize that Halloween is perhaps the only official time of year that grownups give themselves permission to play? Adults now spend more money on all the hoopla associated with that celebration than on any other holiday but Christmas. Yes Halloween recently overtook Valentine's Day for second place. So once a year, on October 31st, we give ourselves license to dress up in wild costumes, wear crazy makeup, organize fun parties, and just have a blast. But what about the other 364 days of the year?

The athletes among us may golf, go bowling, or play softball or touch football from time to time. Often we forget this is a play activity and that it's supposed to be fun. When we find ourselves heaving the golf club or getting upset because our bowling score dipped from the previous week, perhaps we're not approaching things the best way. You see, play is about participation. It's not about winning or losing. It's about having a good time and sharing it with people you like. Do you play poker for the money you may win or for a sense of community?

Sometimes I bet you don't even realize that you *are* at play. I believe gardening (if you really love to garden) is a form of play. I think cooking, if you enjoy scouring cookbooks and food magazines for exciting new recipes that you may want to prepare, is a play activity. Are you a reader? You can't wait to get home to pick up that novel, biography, or self-help book you were immersed in last night? This may be your bliss and, I believe, is a matter of play. Movie going, talking on the phone to a good friend, dining out at a new restaurant, following your favorite TV soap operas, anticipating and experiencing a wonderful night of sex with someone special—this is all play.

Consider these four basic questions: Are you having fun in your life? What do you do when you get stressed? Do you have a good balance between the things you need to do (your job, your family) and your recreation time? Do you take time just to play?

If you don't do it enough, I'm going to give you permission to play right now!

- Take a half hour and go to the park and get on the swings.
- If you loved climbing trees as a kid, find a safe sturdy one and climb, at least to the first branch.
- When was the last time you rode on a Ferris wheel or a merry-go-round? Is there one nearby?

And I'm going to give you permission to play on the weekends or after work as well. Go out and play tennis, or golf, or participate in whatever other sport appeals to you. Just be careful how you approach these games—and I'm not talking about the possibility of injuries. Often we fall into that "grownup trap" that Calvin's dad in the comic strip was talking about. You know—keeping records to quantify our performance. "My golf handicap is coming down." "Remember, good buddy, how I aced you on the tennis court last week!"

We truly have a lot to learn from our children, our nephews and nieces, and the youngsters on the block. All of us were once kids. Do you remember? Take a moment now to reflect on what it was like for us when we were young. We would go outside and meet up with our friends to play "Hide and Seek" or "Giant Steps," or pretend we were "Cops and Robbers," or "Pirates" in search of a grand adventure. Even when we participated in team sports we usually forgot the final score right after it was over. We didn't have to win to have a good time. It was in the participation that the fun and joy appeared.

But now we're adults. Unfortunately most of us were told at a certain age, usually as we entered or graduated from college that the fun was over, that it was time to get serious, that we had to grow up. The message for many of us was that we shouldn't laugh too often, and we certainly couldn't allow ourselves to have a good time anymore.

Why not make your life a game? Why not realize that your day can really be fun? How about "playing" with all the responsibilities and the pitfalls that show up? This mindset offers exciting and rewarding challenges. Studies have shown that people who have fun and enjoy what they're doing tend to be more productive, more effective, and more alive. Actor/Director/Producer Warren Beatty once said, "I love my work and it shows."

PLAY AND THE WORKPLACE

The astonishing truth is that never before has this need for play been more apparent than in the workplace. The business climate has changed dramatically. New corporate practices are causing CEOs and their rank and file employees to experience increasing amounts of job stress. Most people are having less fun at work and reduced company morale is having a profound effect on the bottom line.

Mergers, hostile takeovers, and down-sizing are undermining job security. New concepts of job hiring—getting rid of the higher paid middle-aged managers and replacing them with younger, less experienced, and poorer paid individuals—are becoming the rule.

Computers allow information to be accessed faster and faster, and email, cell phones, faxes, and beepers mandate that we respond to communications almost instantly. The competition of the global economy is taking its toll.

Thankfully, organizations are finding ways to deal with this heightened stress. Companies are creating "wellness" programs, teaching employees about the benefits of healthier eating and the dangers of alcohol, drugs, and smoking. Classes in meditation, yoga, and aerobics provide some relief. Organizational development specialists search out seminars and training that emphasize team-building and mentoring strategies as a way of retaining cohesion among the ranks.

IT'S TIME FOR RECESS

Finally, a lot of these business cultures are listening to what I, and pioneers like me, have been saying for several years now. What your employees also need is RECESS—just like when we were young. As children we had more balanced lives. We went to work every day! Yes the classroom was a true working experience. But we had one eye out for the schoolyard because we always knew that sometime during the day we were going to get recess. We were going to be able to put our books down and go outside just so we could have some fun. We would be able to play with our classmates, to laugh with our friends, and to leave the work behind for a period of time. Then, when we returned to the classroom, we would be refreshed and able to once again put our best effort forward at our desk.

We need RECESS more than ever before!

CHAPTER 2

TAKING TIME TO CELEBRATE "BEING ALIVE"

> "The more you praise and celebrate your life,
> the more there is in life to celebrate."
> —Oprah Winfrey, Television Personality (1954-present)

I read somewhere that having fun and playing is "taking time to celebrate being alive." Successful author and speaker Wayne Dyer often reminds his audiences that "we're all going to be dead a long time!" So if it's good to celebrate being alive, and we agree that we *are* going to be dead a long time, using our remaining years wisely becomes crucial, no matter our age.

Let's start by celebrating as much as we can right in the workplace. What a concept! Why must we decide that for 8 to 10 to 12 hours a day at work we can't have fun, we're not supposed to play, we can't celebrate being alive? Seems to me we're cheating ourselves out of something so important and so nurturing for us.

And let's eliminate this TGIF—"Thank God It's Friday"—attitude that echoes through the corporate corridors. Oh, so we've finally reached the point in the week when we can actually start thinking about the fun and joy of the weekend! My desire is to see all of this celebrating reversed. Let's start hearing "T-G-I-M!" Yes that's right—"Thank God It's Monday"—because we get to go back to work and we're going to make it a good time!

Through the years many great thinkers have shared the belief that work and play must co-exist. Greek writer Anacharis, who lived around 600 B.C., said, "Play so that you can be serious." Shakespeare in his drama, *The Taming of the Shrew*, has one of his characters offer, "No profit grows where there is no pleasure taken." French dramatist Moliere echoed those sentiments when he wrote,

"Our minds need relaxation, and give way
Unless we mix with work a little play."

Spanish-American philosopher George Santayana, in the early 1900s stated, "To the art of working well a civilized race would add the art of playing well." And what about that very common expression, "All work and no play makes Jack a dull boy," we have all heard so many times? When do you think that was written? At the dawn of the Industrial Revolution? During the Depression? Take a guess. Come on, take a guess. Play along. Perhaps you'll be amazed to learn that English writer James Howell wrote that way back in the 1600s!

Now I'm not suggesting you have to select one at the expense of the other. I'm not implying that work is bad and play is good. I love my work. I'll never retire. I love reminding people to "play." I love facilitating my "playshops." And that is my work, my wonderful work. All I'm saying, and you'll hear it many times in this book, is that you need to play as well.

On several occasions I have done "playshops" for clients of The Wellness Community. This is a nationwide organization that provides psychological support for people and their families who are dealing with cancer. Each time we played for almost three hours and everyone seemed to have a fine time. I volunteer my services to groups like that after I learned that play, and the fun and laughter it elicits, is very important in dealing with and combating illnesses and pain.

Dr. Carl Simonton, the cancer specialist I talked about in the introduction, feels that play lifts the spirits of cancer patients with advanced malignancy. In an issue of *Prevention* magazine he was quoted as saying:

> "The first thing a person does when he finds out he's ill is to stop playing. It shouldn't be that way. Play is mandatory, not elective. Playing is an activity that tends to produce emotions of joy and the experience of having

fun. Feeling joyful and feeling like having fun increase our energy. Playing also mobilizes our desire to live because life becomes more meaningful."

Dr. David Bresler, a psychiatrist, who helps people deal with pain, in the same article states: "People who come to me in pain tell me how they used to have fun, how they used to dance, how they used to go to the movies. I tell them that the reason they have pain is because they don't do those things anymore. Pain isn't the cause, it's the result."

He imparts to his patients a wide range of self-management techniques designed to optimize and maximize the body's inner ability to cope more effectively with pain. Like Norman Cousins, he espouses the importance of laughter and play in stimulating the endorphin system. Endorphins are the body's natural pain relievers which can produce a euphoric or even tranquilizing effect. As Carl Simonton likes to say, "I don't laugh because I'm happy. I'm happy because I laugh."

In that same article, Dr. Simonton brings up a whole other issue. He claims that if we overwork and underplay, we tend to feel depressed. But if we overplay and underwork, we feel fearful that we are ignoring our responsibilities.

So once again it's a matter of balance. We must find time to do both. Because, without play, we don't get the chance to truly enjoy our life and to fully "celebrate being alive."

CHAPTER 3

THE MOST CREATIVE PEOPLE ARE PLAYFUL

> "The creation of something new is not accomplished by the intellect but by the play instinct acting from inner necessity. The creative mind plays with the objects it loves."
> —Carl Jung, Swiss Psychiatrist (1875-1961)

Unfortunately many people don't think they approach their jobs in a creative way. At my seminars when I ask participants if they think they're "creative" many don't believe so. They may have embraced a faulty concept.

For instance, I have an older brother who has always been able to draw well. By the time he was 10 years old, Joel could duplicate comic strip characters like Dick Tracy and Donald Duck perfectly. So I believed he was creative because he had this talent, but I wasn't because I couldn't draw like he could.

When I went to school and saw other kids sit down and begin to play the piano or be selected for the glee club because of their unique singing voices I decided they were creative—they had a talent. But since I couldn't sing or play a musical instrument I wasn't creative.

A few years ago Sylvia Woodside, at the time Human Resources Manager for the Los Angeles District of the U.S. Postal Service (who hired me many times to do programs for her troops) sent me an article from the magazine, *Personal Selling Power*. It was written by English actor John Cleese, one of the founding members of the Monty Python group. Following that success he formed a company to write and produce novel training films. In the course of that work he studied the creative process and how it impacted on personal and business relationships and productivity. In the article he mentioned a psychologist named Donald MacKinnon, who had once been a researcher at the University of California at Berkeley.

According to Cleese, MacKinnon had come to believe that:

> "Creativity is not a talent, it is a way of operating—a mode of behaving. Donald MacKinnon described the particular facility as 'an ability to play.' Indeed, he described the most creative people as being child-like for they were able to play with ideas, to explore them, not for any immediate purpose, but just for the enjoyment of playing, the delight of exploration."

So let's contemplate what it is to be a child, and how, for example, a five- or six-year-old behaves. What are the qualities that they manifest? In no particular order we know that they are curious and love to examine objects of nature to find out more about them. That seems to go hand in hand with their inquisitive nature—they are always asking questions, many of which grownups perhaps can't answer. Ever had a child relentlessly ask you why the sky is blue?

Children are energetic. They are always on the go, first into this and then that. They can run circles around their adult counterparts. They are also joyful. Remember that statistic—on average they laugh and smile more than 200 times a day. Kids are imaginative. Ask them to play a game with you and for them to be in charge. Then listen as they tell you who you are and what you're supposed to be doing in the situation they have just set up.

Young ones are adventurous. Unless you put stops on them they usually want to try new things without realizing any potential danger. "Let me climb that tree; I want to cross that street now; just let me run free." These are the wishes of the child. They also tend to be honest. How many parents have been embarrassed when your child announced out loud in the supermarket that the person in the next line was "really fat" or "has only one arm?" They are emotional too. You always know when a child is happy (lots of laughter and glee); sad (the tears are instantaneous), and angry (watch out for the block that is about to be thrown across the room). Children are spontaneous; they're accepting; they're magical, and they like to have fun!

If more of us could approach our jobs with this childlike verve we would bring new energy, curiosity, joyfulness, imagination, adventure, emotion, honesty, spontaneity, acceptance and even magic to what we do. And the businesses we work for would be rewarded with more productive, happy employees.

That wonderful anthropologist Ashley Montagu, author of such books as *Growing Young, The Natural Superiority Of Women,* and *The Elephant Man,* who I will be speaking about at length later in this book, once created a short quiz to determine just how in-touch an adult was in his neotenous or childlike qualities. It might interest you to know where you stand on that scale. In Chapter 28 you can take that test just to ease your curiosity.

CHAPTER 4

CLOSE YOUR EYES AND LET'S TAKE A TRIP

"When you finally go back to your old hometown, you find it wasn't the old home you missed but your childhood."
—*Sam Ewing, Writer (1920-2001)*

Remember as a child what it was like to run free with your playmates? Do you recall your favorite games or the toys you liked to play with? Let me provide you with a powerful memory from your past. In a moment I'm going to ask you to put down this book and close your eyes. Then I will want you to envision yourself as a child, coming home from school after a hard day of learning. Perhaps you will see yourself changing into your play clothes. You may remember a favorite pair of blue jeans from your childhood. Then see yourself at play. Look at your face. Are you having a good time? Are you laughing? And who are you with? You may see the faces of kids you haven't thought about in years. So put the book down now and close your eyes and take yourself back to your childhood, when the most important thing that mattered was having some fun at play.

DO YOUR CLOSED EYES EXERCISE NOW (5-6 MINUTES)

What was that like? Are you smiling at remembering the things you used to do as a child? Where were you? In the backyard? On the front stoop of your apartment house? Were you roller skating down the block, or riding your bicycle? Had you and your buddies organized a game of softball in the schoolyard, or were you and your girlfriends jumping rope? Did you see the faces of childhood friends? Did you zero in on games or toys that you had forgotten about? Do you wish you knew what happened to some of those kids from your neighborhood?

In the seminar, after several moments to conjure up their scenes, I start to bring participants out of their reverie. I ask them to open their eyes and return to the present moment. I often notice that some people don't really want to open their eyes, wishing to remain back in their childhoods. Then I ask for volunteers to share with the group "where they were." Hands always shoot up into the air. People seem to want to relate their individual memories of playing as a kid.

They may have seen themselves climbing up a tree or playing "stick ball" in the street; jumping rope with their girl friends or tobogganing down a hill. Or they were running through the streets in a spirited game of "Hide and Seek" or creating a make-believe scenario in a game of "House" or "Doctor." Whatever the tale, it's most often a joyous remembrance for them. They have no trouble describing where they were, what they were doing, what clothes they had on, and who they were with. Often it's a long forgotten playmate.

Today, as grownups we almost never get "recess." I have done my programs before thousands and thousands of people and not once has anyone reported that their boss ever came into their office, or stopped by their desk and said, "You've been working too hard! Why don't you just go outside and take recess!!"

Never happens, never. But the truth is that everyone of us needs recess during our working hours. We need to slow down for awhile, to put ourselves in a place where we can have some fun, participate in some play activity for a period of time. As when we were kids, it replenishes our energies, it de-stresses us, it gives us some comfort. Now I'm not suggesting that Corporate America should build recess into every day (though that would be nice), but I am suggesting that all of us need to take care of ourselves several times a day. We can even provide recess for ourselves without leaving our office, or even getting up from our desks.

One of those ways is to just close your eyes when you're

feeling stressed or overworked. Perhaps when you've had a contentious conversation on the phone and now you're feeling that you want to react but know that the reaction could be disastrous. With your eyes closed you can go back in time to your childhood and see yourself at play, like the exercise you just completed. Or else, with your eyes closed, you can relive the vacation you took earlier this year. See yourself visiting all those wonderful monuments and museums, or flying over volcanoes, or eating in that fabulous French restaurant in Paris. What fun, what play!

Conversely, you can pre-experience the vacation you're planning for next year. Try and imagine what it will be like, what some of the cities or countries will be offering; who you might meet along the way. You will realize you can hardly wait—though you must. But you are "playing" with ideas of what the vacation may be. With your eyes closed your mind can block out the negative situation you have just endured and replace it with something pleasurable.

I have used this exercise to good advantage whenever I visit my dentist's office. When I was a youngster I had such bad teeth that every time I had a dental checkup it usually revealed 6 to 10 cavities. Unfortunately my childhood dentist didn't believe in Novocain! So the entire drilling procedure was very scary and very painful.

The little child in my head is still traumatized by that early experience, still remembers the whirling drill and the immense pain. So he usually shows up when I'm visiting my dentist, Bruce Edwards, who happens to be a terrific dentist and a nice man. Still the voice says, "This time it could be scary. It might be painful just like when we were a kid."

So to ease my "child's fear" I just close my eyes and go somewhere else while Dr. Edwards is preparing my mouth for a crown or doing some high-speed drilling. For me it could be my childhood (but not at that *other* dentist's office), or my last vacation, or my next vacation, or even a recent sexual experience! The idea here is to put oneself in a play-like setting—that setting is completely up to you!

CHAPTER 5

CHILDHOOD NEVER LETS GO OF US

"In every real man a child is hidden that wants to play."
—*Friedrich Nietzsche, German Philosopher (1844-1900)*

My "playshops" are a way of getting people on their feet to rediscover the joy of cooperative play. They prove what the German philosopher Friederich Nietzsche said over 100 years ago. Now Nietzsche was a bit of a chauvinist as many men of his time. So I have added the concept that in every *real woman* also is a child hidden who wants to play!

Playing transports us back to our childhoods in a most marvelous way. English author J.B. Priestley supported this notion when he wrote: "Indeed, now that I come to think of it, I never really feel grownup at all. Perhaps this is because childhood, catching our imagination when it is fresh and tender, never lets go of us."

More recent is the comment by Academy Award®-winning Peter Jackson, the acclaimed director of the *Lord of the Rings* trilogy, who on accepting the Modern Master award at the Santa Barbara Film Festival laughed and said, "Me a Modern Master? That's so funny. All I'm doing is what I did as a child—just using my imagination to come up with creative ideas."

Do you recall Julie Taymor's words in accepting a Tony Award® for directing the Broadway theatrical musical, *The Lion King*? She exclaimed: "I was lucky. I had parents who let me play, play, play!"

In our childhood we had important work to do. It was called play. It was where we learned about the world; where we created lives and roles for ourselves; where we practiced how to deal with others; where we got so involved with our activities that we lost all track of time, suffered less stress, laughed, romped, and cavorted.

This I endeavor to do in these seminars. The payoff for me is to see grownups return, if for a fleeting moment, to their childhoods. The smiling faces, the laughing, the glee—the living in the moment that play inspires. It is very powerful stuff and I am delighted that I can help to make it happen.

The payoff for the participants is that they are re-introduced to the part of themselves that is still a kid. It's the voice within that constantly talks to us. So as they participate in these programs they feel energized and very satisfied. It's as if they took a little child who was "at them" all day, wanting to play, actually out to the playground to have that wish fulfilled. They learn new things about themselves; they learn new things about their colleagues (who are also showing up as their inner child). Often they find a new vision for their work. It's very powerful stuff!

CHAPTER 6

DR. PLAY'S FAVORITE GAMES

"In our play we reveal what kind of people we are."
—*Ovid, Greek Author (43 B.C.-17 A.D.)*

My form of recess consists of a series of interactive games and activities that are a lot of fun and also teach people (if they are receptive) to see how their approach to the games can be helpful back in the workplace. Some of the activities are very verbal; some not. Many get the participants moving around the room, but they are not sporting events that require special skills. Lots of the games have exotic titles such as: "You Can't Fool Us," "Knots," "Face Pass," "Television," "Magic #14," "Aura," "Incorporations," "Fruit Basket," "Squirrels In The Trees," "Giants, Elves And Wizards," "A What?," and "Car/Car." You can find a full description of the way many of these games are played in Part 5 of this book.

    Once we have played I provide an extensive "debriefing" of what has really gone on while we played. The games are actually metaphors for how we act and react to things in our daily rounds. Some of the activities explore trust. Certainly trust issues abound in the workplace and with professional organizations. Certain games ask the participants to take risks or to be flexible in their approach. There are situations in which the group needs to be fully connected to accomplish a goal. Some of the events deal with acknowledgement, commitment and support. All of the activities reveal commonalities, spark creativity and certainly stimulate laughter and joy.

    In my questions after the games I ask the participants to reflect on their experience:

- Were you flexible?
- Did you need to feel in control?
- Was your instinct to be competitive?
- Did the issue of right and wrong come up?
- Were you involved in problem-solving as you played?
- Did you try to lead or were you a follower?
- How did you feel playing the non-verbal games?
- Was any game frustrating to you and why?
- Did you ever get "performance anxiety" while playing?
- How good were your powers of observation in the games?
- Was it okay to feel totally silly sometimes?
- Were you surprised by something a colleague did?
- Were the closed-eyes games and exercises scary to you?
- Did you ever feel judged?

Important information is reported during this part of the seminar. The games certainly provide challenges to the players. Here is a brief description of some of my favorite ones and what happened at times while we were playing.

WHEN'S YOUR BIRTHDAY?

It is sometimes a challenging game for it requires people to communicate without speaking. This is extremely hard for some individuals and it gives them the opportunity to see what gifts their power of speech provides. We arrange a single row of chairs in a line with one person to each chair. I explain that soon all the participants will be asked to get up and to re-organize themselves according to their birthday. The person whose birthday is closest to January 1st will sit in Chair #1 and the person whose natal day is nearest December 31st will sit in the last chair in the row, with everyone else arranged in between. But they're not allowed to talk or write anything down on paper. Everyone is motioned to get up and work (or play) together as a team in configuring the correct order. Most people start using hand and finger gestures to communicate. Others do imaginary writing on the palm of their hand. Some reach for their wallets to reveal their date of birth as shown on their driver's license.

I always remind the group that "playing" is never about right or wrong (just participation) and then I go into phase two, walking down the line and asking people when their birthday is, to see how well the group has done. But I have one proviso—if we find someone out of place, no one in the group is allowed to point at them and go "Ooh!" This always brings a laugh from the crowd, reminding them how as children they may have loved to point out the failing of others. In almost every seminar one, two or maybe three people will be out of place, especially when a large group is playing the game. Almost always, in mock defiance, someone will utter the dreaded "Ooh!" but I see that as being playful now rather than punitive. On the few occasions where everyone has selected the appropriate seat, you can't imagine the cheers that go up when the group realizes they have all navigated the game successfully. We still like to win, don't we?

Once when I was conducting a seminar for the loan department of a bank, one of the executives revealed that "When's Your Birthday?" had made her mad.

"Mad? Why were you mad?" I inquired. I had never gotten that kind of response to the game before.

"Because some of the people were not playing the game *right!*" was her swift answer.

"But remember I told all of you that playing these games is not about right or wrong. It's just participating."

"I know, I know," she responded. "And I believe that I am the type of manager who allows those who report to me to use their own measures to do the job, so I really need to explore why I was so disturbed."

Another aspect of this game is to see who is a team player and who is not. Do they just take care of themselves and figure out where they belong, or do they try to see if other people in the group are aligning themselves with the people around them? Sometimes after someone has figured out the two people they should be sitting between they'll get up from their chair and work the line to see if others are also following suit.

There are also the wanderers who may be using their fingers to signal like everyone else but don't really try to get anyone's attention. Often they find the wrong seat simply because they didn't go the extra step to engage in a communication with others in the group. In the workplace they're often the ones who like to do their own thing.

Add to this the reticent ones who just feel odd trying to connect with others in this different way, give up almost instantly, and merely sit down in any open seat. Once in a while you have someone who just didn't listen to the rules at all. Guess if they eventually get to the right place!

YOUR MOST MEMORABLE BIRTHDAY
In this activity I organize the group into pairs and ask them to speak to each other about "The Most Memorable Birthday You Ever Had."

I further suggest they "make believe" they're either Geraldo Rivera or Barbara Walters and literally interview their partner to get the complete story.

"For those of you who are pretending to be Barbara Walters," I playfully add, "see if you can make your partner cry," a method Barbara has become noted for on her television Specials. That always draws lots of laughter from my knowing audiences.

Once they're finished with the stories I ask for volunteers to relate the story that was just told to them. The fact that a storyteller in each couplet now gets to be the passive listener for the rest of the group's amusement and edification is a surprise. I'm always interested in knowing afterwards whether this unexpected attention and acknowledgement was pleasurable or uncomfortable. So many people try to hide who they are, or feel unworthy, or really want to be known but don't ever feel anyone cares. It gives the participants a chance to think about their reactions while their "most memorable birthday" story is being told.

There are other things to be learned as well. I ask the participants if they enjoyed telling their story or hearing their partner's story more. I want to know if they think it is okay to learn something significant about a co-worker that doesn't relate to their business relationship. A few other questions:

- Was your partner excited about telling his or her story to you?

- Did that surprise you?
- Were you excited or a little hesitant to tell your story to them?
- When your partner told your story to the whole group did they make it more dramatic or funnier than the way you told it?

KNOTS

This is a game of connection where groups of eight form into a tightly knit circle, extend both hands into the middle and, grasping another hand with each of their hands, literally create one large knot. The object of the game is to untie the knot without letting go of any hand. It is truly a game of commitment and a fun event. People in the circle guide each other along. One suggests that two members holding hands lower their bodies and arms so that someone else in the circle can step over the arms and untie that portion of the knot.

The circles that finish before the others may feel very superior, as if they have won a game. But I have cautioned those groups over and over that the games are not competitions. As they stand around watching the slower groups still going through the process of untying the knot I explain that these remaining groups are actually *getting to play longer* than those just standing around. It's a different and yet apt perception of the circumstances. And it gives me a chance to remind the assembled once again that the pure nature of play is not winning —it's participation.

This game illustrates something else too. The individuals get a chance to see if they are a leaders or a followers, and how that resonates for them. Certain members of each knotted group usually take charge of organizing the untangling. Most often they are senior management and they're used to making decisions. Very rarely will a junior employee take on that role. So the picture I witness is of a few individuals verbally directing the group, while others play a passive role.

In the debriefing I like to discuss this phenomenon as a powerful metaphor for the office. I ask the participants to reflect on the role they chose during that game. I want to know if that's the way they show up at department meetings. I suggest that the leaders try something different next time they're holding a conference. Rather than always feeling that they have to come up with solutions, they might sit back and elicit discussion from the junior members. They might hear some good ideas they hadn't thought about. This is a good way for managers to enlist the aid of their troops. In reverse it's also a call to the novices to put themselves out there, to take a risk, and to share what their solution might be. They might even benefit from their suggestions.

CAR/CAR
The rules of Car/Car are that two people pair up and one acts as the Car while the other is the Driver. The Driver maneuvers the Car through the group of other cars by putting his or her hands on the Car's shoulder and moving him or her forward, backward and from side to side. All the while the Car must keep his or her eyes closed! This is a game of trust because the Car does not know where it's going and must rely on the Driver to give it a safe ride.

Once during a program for Xerox, one of the participants expressed the fear she felt as she was playing this game. She believed that her Driver was moving her around too fast and that it was very scary. I asked her why she just didn't tell her Driver to move a little more slowly. No rule exists in the game that prevents a Car from talking to his or her Driver. She said she couldn't do that because she was being "driven" around the room by her boss, the head of the department, and felt she would be out of line to say something. As we discussed this further, all of a sudden she exclaimed, "Wait a second. Maybe the way he was speeding me around the room was a message!"

"A message? What kind of message?" I inquired.

"Well maybe he was suggesting that I'm not moving fast enough here at Xerox, or that I'm capable of doing more. Perhaps he thinks I could have a more senior position in this department than simply being his secretary!"

As she was saying this I looked over at her boss who had a bemused look on his face. I couldn't really determine if he was agreeing with her assessment or not and I never found out. But the mere fact that all of this came up for her while we were playing our fun and silly game of Car/Car showed me that the games do engender deeper feelings and new ways of potential learning.

So, just as in childhood, our play can bring an individual critical awareness along with pure moments of joy.

CHAPTER 7

JUST CALL ME "TEX," AND WHAT DO I CALL YOU?

"Just play. Have fun. Enjoy the game."
—Michael Jordan, Professional Athlete (1963-present)

Because I've learned that it is hard to get some people up to play, I have devised what I think is a novel way for them to feel less self-conscious and motivated to participate.

At the end of my opening talk, as I introduce the games part of the program, I explain that all the participants will need to wear name tags because I will be addressing some of them individually, and that I don't yet know their names.

I tell them I will be wearing a name tag as well, but it will not say "Howard." That's because as a kid, I disliked that name. Though I was growing up on the streets of New York City, in my imaginary world I longed to be known as "Tex"—my childhood wish to be a cowboy! With that pronouncement I remove a previously prepared "Tex" name tag from my shirt pocket and proudly stick it on my chest. Then I declare that I have taken the liberty of preparing a vast array of "nickname" tags for the participants, and direct them to a designated table in the room where I have laid out the different names. I ask them to choose a name that "jumps out at them."

It is a great ice breaker. Some people actually run to the table, instantly see the nickname they want, and grab it before anyone else can. Others study the myriad names and finally spot the one they most like. For those who continue to have trouble selecting a name, I suggest that they let the "little kid" inside them make the choice. That usually helps.

Before long I am surrounded by "Lucky," "Elvis," "Diva,"

"Lambchop," "Princess," "Magic," "Jock," "Gidget," "Zorro," "Peaches," "Foxy," "Babycakes," "Rainbow," and on and on.

What's most important is that the participants are already laughing and wondering why their fellow employees, friends, or colleagues have selected the nicknames that are now plastered to their chests. Later in the session they will get a chance to intermingle with others in the group and find out why they picked the names they did. Wonderful stories emerge. Though some people weren't really sure why they picked out their particular nickname, by the end of the session most of them have a very logical explanation.

If it's "Batman," "Roadrunner," "Bullwinkle," "Klingon," "Tabatha," or "Gilligan," it's usually tied to their favorite television character or show they watched when they were a kid.

When they choose names like "Party Animal," "Spitfire," "Audacious," "Live One!" or "Maverick," it usually relates to how they define their personalities.

Someone who has selected "Mermaid" may have competed as a swimmer in school or simply likes the water. "Cowabunga" usually is a giveaway for a current or former surfer.

Others select names simply because they think they sound funny or playful such as "Bubba," "Shlep," "Humantosh," "Eek," or "Gorgonzola."

People who are big music fans might pick "Aretha," "Garth," "Dead Head," "Aerosmith," "Reba," "Beethoven" or simply "Music."

Sports fanatics may go for "Jogger," "Ali," "Hoopster," "Golfer," or even "Zamboni," the name of the machine that manufactures new ice between hockey periods.

Others may indicate their inner wish for financial success by choosing "Lottery," "Megabucks," "Porsche," or even "Ivana."

Fans of the movies can be spotted—"Hollywood," "Groucho," "Whoopi," "Demi," "Rhett," "Denzel," "Keanu" and "Bardot" are common.

Selecting names like "Bard," "Wolfgang," "Steinbeck," "Chopin," "Ulysses," or "Michaelangelo" may connote lovers of the arts.

Foodies like to go for "Fudge," "Taffy," "Popsicle," "Salsa," "Macaroni," "Hoagie," or "Double Latte."

Others may be proud of their hometowns or the parts of the country they hail from. "Toledo," "Jersey," "Dallas," "Georgia," "Pasadena," and "Brooklyn" are often seen on participants' chests. Or maybe it's destinations that they have visited or would like to go to such as "Maui," "Nantucket," or "Versailles."

I'm not the only one who fancies himself a cowboy or Western fan. "Lone Ranger," "Buckaroo," "Hopalong," "Whipper Snapper," or even "Outlaw" are crowd favorites.

Toys, games, and childhood places to play seem to resonate. "Hula Hoop," "Sandbox," "Tinker Toy," "Barbie," "Circus," "Monkey Bars," and "Hopscotch" are sometimes chosen.

Dog lovers have picked names such as "Snoopy," "Bow Wow," "Lassie," "Pooch," "Dalmatian," or simply "Puppy Face."

Other animal lovers can choose from names like "Kitten," "Otter," "Orca," "Tiger," "Koala," "Rhino," and "Rats."

One of my favorite things to do after the seminar is to ask people why they chose the names they did. Often I know what their answer will be, but sometimes I am very surprised.

"I'm left-handed too," I said to a fellow wearing the name tag "Lefty."

"Oh I'm not left-handed," he replied.

I was curious. "So why did you pick that name?"

"It's my politics!" he responded, breaking into a broad smile.

A guy in one playshop selected the name "Popcorn." His explanation, "It's something so closed up and then we cook it and it opens up." He had had some initial reservations about participating in one of my community programs, but attended at the urging of a friend of mine. Now he felt (like the corn kernel) that he had been liberated. His parting words to me that morning were, "Great fun!"

Another participant in that same program had chosen the nickname "Dixie." Revealing her real name to be "Ula," she offered, "I always wanted a name that ended with an 'E' sound. All names that end in 'E' sound so cute." That day she could also have picked "Bunny," "Cookie," "Daisy," "Fluffy," "Angie," "Gigi" and on and on.

Then there was the time in February of 1994 when I did a program for the Los Angeles District of the United States Postal Service. The Winter Olympics were in full swing at the time and I had spiced up my selection of names with "Ski," "Hockey Puck," "Tonya" (how can we forget the troubled Tonya Harding?), and "Bonnie"—in salute to America's champion speed skater, Bonnie Blair.

At the end of the session one of the managers approached to tell me how delighted she was to see that name tag "Bonnie" displayed. She went on to explain that she grabbed it before anybody else could. She now wore it proudly on her dress.

"I imagine you've been watching the Olympics?"

"No," she replied, looking a bit confused.

"I thought, perhaps, you were a fan of speed skater Bonnie Blair?"

"No, no, this is in honor of my father. His nickname was 'Bonny,' spelled with a 'Y'. He died last year and I miss him so much. But he was the person who always played with me when I was a child. I really wanted *this* name tag!"

CHAPTER 8

BLUE GLASSES' REBELLION AND OTHER STRANGE TALES

> "If you wait for the perfect moment when all is safe and assured, it may never arrive. Mountains will not be climbed, races won, or lasting happiness achieved."
> —Maurice Chevalier, French Entertainer (1888-1972)

There are three specific behavior types who show up at a LET'S PLAY AGAIN seminar. One group I call the "competitors." These individuals were confident athletes in their younger days, or at least the kind of kids who willingly and freely jumped into school activities without any coaxing. They're ready to participate in the games—in fact they're ready to "go" and want me to stop talking and to let the games begin.

One or two individuals in almost every group I have branded the "cynics," because that's exactly who they are! They have decided that they don't want to play, and that they're going to be very resistant if they're asked to participate. They are already grimacing, or growling, and making their feelings known through their facial expressions and their body language.

By far the largest group is what I deem the "cautious ones." As children they probably had to be invited to play. Perhaps they were concerned about their athletic ability and thought they would be embarrassed if the play turned competitive. It's not that they don't want to be part of the fun; they simply want to know everything beforehand. This will help them decide whether they're equal to the challenge, and whether ultimately they'll have the kind of good time I promise upfront.

In the early days of my life as a motivational speaker, I conducted a program for some executives at a resort hotel. Months before, the head of Human Resources had experienced my work at a meeting of a professional association, and felt this was exactly the kind of team-building program needed by her senior management group.

The seminar went exceedingly well and I was invited to join the group as they headed down the street to a neighborhood hangout for a late buffet supper. I always hope I will be asked to attend these post-events because then I get a chance to interact with the attendees and get any feedback they wish to offer.

Moseying up to me on the food line was one of the executives, who I recalled had been one of the more reserved participants.

"I enjoyed your seminar very much," she said.

"Thank you," I replied.

"There's a particular reason I'm telling you this," she continued. I awaited a further explanation. I knew one was coming.

"When Barbara (the Director of Human Resources) suggested to the management committee, which I am a member of, that we invite you to lead tonight's seminar, and then told us something about your techniques, I was against it. I felt it didn't have a place as part of our executive get-togethers. Perhaps I was scared, I'm not sure, but I just didn't want to be part of it."

I said nothing. I just kept listening.

"But I was outvoted. And do you know what? Now I'm glad, because this seminar was very good for me. I'm usually very reserved and this broke some walls down for me. So I want to thank you."

There have been other occasions when I have received resistance from participants. One of them occurred during an evening early in my Dr. Play career. I was substituting for Bob Maurer, the gifted Los Angeles psychologist who does powerful lectures on the topic of "success." Needing to be out of town for a long-standing engagement, he had asked me to be his guest replacement, and had "hyped" my play seminars to his class. I showed up that night and found a sizeable group of men and women expecting a traditional lecture. I immediately put that notion to rest, explaining how my evening would be an interactive, experiential program. Most seemed to get excited by that prospect, and put down their notebooks—except for one woman who approached me during the break, just as we were moving into the games part of the program.

"I will not be playing," she stated. "I'm going to stay seated and just take notes."

I tried to explain that note taking wasn't really necessary; that the learning came from the active play. She was not convinced.

"I simply will not participate and I'm giving you the courtesy of telling you up front," she countered.

Rather than get into an argument I responded that if that's what she really wanted to do it would be fine. All the while, however, I was chuckling inside. Here standing before me was this brightly attired sixty-plus-year-old woman. And resting on her nose were the wildest pair of *neon blue* horn-rimmed glasses I had ever seen. They even outdid former talk show host Sally Jessy Raphael's famous red ones. I kept thinking to myself, "With a get-up like that, this woman obviously has a lot of kid in her, and she's telling me she doesn't want to play? Let's see how long that lasts."

My instincts couldn't have been more correct! She sat through the first game but as I organized the group for the next, she put down her note pad, jumped to her feet, and declared that she had changed her mind and would indeed be joining the rest of her colleagues. It was clear to me that here was someone who had needed to fully check out "the scene" before she would feel safe in the activities. And once she started playing with the rest of the group she gave of herself wholeheartedly.

At the end of the evening she approached me, declaring she had had a great time, and then offered her card and suggested I call. She wanted to set me up with some other organizations she belonged to that she felt would get value out of my seminar. So go figure!

Asking people—who don't like to take risks—to do just that, is a hard proposition. It is certainly difficult for me in areas of my life. But when I undertake those seemingly frightening obstacles, and when I find out that I am equal to the occasion, or haven't "died" in the attempt, it is always a very freeing feeling. And it was so for the hotel executive and "Ms. Blue Glasses." On their particular evenings of play they took risks and were liberated from fearful considerations and self doubts. And I'm so glad to have played a part in their growth as human beings!

CHAPTER 9

THE DAY OF THE IGUANA

"Be kind, for everyone you meet is fighting a hard battle."
—*Plato, Greek Philosopher (427-347 B.C.)*

Sometimes while I'm conducting a training program, issues come up for people that are totally unexpected. As I've mentioned previously, the word "play" can conjure up fearful feelings for some individuals. They have questions and may show some resistance: "What are we going to be playing?" "Is this an athletic thing?" "I was never good at sports!" "I never played as a child and I'm not going to start now!" "I don't want to appear silly or foolish in front of my colleagues, so I'd rather not participate."

Because of this I often tell the organizer of the event (usually the training manager, the director of organizational development, or the head of human resources) to leave the title of my company off the official agenda. I suggest instead that they just mention my name and explain that I will do a program devoted to stress management and team-building. I prefer to ease into the play element in stages, once I have the trust of the participants.

One of my earliest clients, the United States Postal Service, used to do a great deal of training. A lot of it was good but I did witness a few poorly planned and utterly boring seminars. That is why some postal workers have walked into my rooms apprehensively. Sometimes their initial reactions have even bordered on hostility. The faces and body language seem to be asking, "Why do I have to be here and sit through something that's probably going to be a waste of my time?"

This realization always causes me to laugh internally because I know what I've prepared, and how enjoyable and energizing it's going to be for them. I've already envisioned how delighted the participants are going to feel when it's over. And there have been countless occasions when burly men have come up to me at the close of a session, literally wanting to hug me because they felt so good!

But a few years ago, while I was doing a program for a middle-management group, something quite disturbing happened that I will remember for the rest of my life. I was in the part of my seminar when I ask participants to close their eyes as I take them on that guided imagery trip back to their childhood. Everybody immediately got comfortable in their seats and closed their eyes—except one woman in the last row who was glaring at me and shaking her head vigorously from side to side. She was letting me know that she was not going to cooperate. Oops, I thought to myself, here is someone who looks very uncomfortable. In the past I would have inquired what the problem was, but this time I decided to leave the situation alone. She sat there, arms now tightly folded over her chest, continuing to peer at me with a very angry expression on her face.

Eventually I introduced the "name tag" portion of the event where, as you recall, everyone gets the chance to select a "play nickname" for the activities part of the program. As the people returned to their seats, excited and laughing and showing each other the names they had picked, I noticed *that* same woman again, sitting now very stiffly, obviously still in major discomfort. This time I decided to inquire.

"You don't look like you're having any fun," I said to the woman in the most playful voice I could muster.

"I hate this crap!" she exploded. "That's why I took *this* name tag," pointing to her chest which sported the name, "Iguana." And then she added, "I feel like biting your head off!"

I was stung by her invective. In that instant I perceived that here was quite a wounded person. I am not a psychologist but I instinctively wanted to know all about her childhood, sensing that what was causing this very negative reaction emanated from a long time ago. Stifling my curiosity and, in the mildest of voices, I said, "Well I'm going to check back with you after we've played and see how you feel then."

Her response: "Well I'm not going to like this at all!"

I proceeded with the games and everyone in the room seemed to be having a grand time. At one point I introduced an activity called, "Matching Symbols," in which four members of the same circle, without speaking, are asked to display one of four different symbols (a fist, one finger, a palm facing up or facing down) to the others in their group. The object is for everyone to match the exact same symbol at the same time. Sometimes groups do it on the first try and squeal with delight. More often the result is a mixed bag of symbols, which makes everyone laugh, and then they try it again until they all match. While the groups were literally "trying their hand" with this game I was circulating around the room as I do regularly. I decided to check on the group that "Iguana" was part of.

"How are you doing?" I inquired.

"She won't play!" was the response of three people pointing at "you know who."

I had "Iguana" step aside and asked why she wasn't participating. She informed me she had no intention of playing. Realizing that I needed to safeguard the fun of everyone else, I said to her, "Listen you have a choice here. You can either decide to play or you can leave because I don't want you to be a disturbing element in the group." She responded that she couldn't leave. "This is mandatory and all my bosses are here."

"So make the choice to stay and get whatever benefit you can out of what is going on," I suggested. She went back to the group and I watched as she made a half-hearted attempt to participate.

The games continued, the fun escalated, and I felt very pleased with what was happening. Finally I asked everyone to sit down so that we could have a debriefing. And as the end of the seminar approached, true to my word, I turned to "Iguana" and asked her if the events had been as bad as she imagined they would be, and whether she had had *any* fun. Her response: "Well it was pretty bad but I would play that 'Car/Car' game again!"

After I had dismissed the group and was packing up, the training department employee who had been my contact for the event hurried over to me. She reported that at first she had not known who the "defiant" person was, and had quietly asked some of the other folks in the room. They had told her that "Iguana" from a rural postal office, was a manager with a nasty reputation. I realized I was being told this so I would feel a little better about the trouble I had had with her.

To the contrary, I felt I had learned a valuable lesson and that "Iguana" had indeed given me a precious gift. You see I would like to have a tremendously positive impact on everyone who attends one of my seminars. But the reality is that people will bring into the room all the attitudes and memories that got them to that day. And play for some people isn't the pleasurable thing it was for many of us while we were growing up. Obviously those bad memories, either consciously or subconsciously, were engaged for "Iguana" that day.

But I did get her to make the attempt. And she did admit there was one game she enjoyed. So I did succeed with "Iguana" on whatever level she was able to open herself to me. And that I think is progress and it is more than okay.

CHAPTER 10

RECESSING RECESS

"To affect the quality of the day, that is the art of life."
—Henry Thoreau, American Writer (1817-1862)

As I have just reported, after we finish the recess or games part of the seminar I ask participants to return to their seats so that we can talk—in essence have a debriefing period. Everyone is always very relaxed, in contrast to the way some of them felt when the program began. The reason: the act of playing has a calming effect on people, especially if the games are not competitive. It is a stress reducer because the activities have required people to be "in the moment" and, when we are in that frame of mind, we become relaxed.

Much of our stress has to do with future or past thinking. When we have deadlines, when we're sitting at our computer and can't find the creativity to do a report that is due, then we are stressed. The "what if" scenario—fear of the future—is a potent fear-producing element of our life. It permeates everything. "What if I can't write the report?" becomes "What if I really can't do the job? What if the person in the next cubicle is better than me? What if my boss really doesn't like me?" You can probably add lots of "what ifs" to that list.

Then, there's the fear of the past—the "I should have," as in "I should have majored in marketing in college. I should have handled that phone conversation differently this morning. I should have listened to my parents. I should have leased the car rather than buying it." When we resort to bringing up the past and start regretting some of the decisions we made along the way, we put ourselves in a stress mode that is futile and non-productive.

Whatever happened in the past is over. We can't change it, so why fret about it and cause ourselves more stress?

Most people are amazed by how quickly the time has flown during a playshop. My programs usually last from three to three-and-a-half hours, and people can't believe they have been there for that period of time. I compare this to the way we often get engrossed in a book. We sit down, start reading, get so involved, that when we next notice the time, we discover it may be an hour or two later. It's the reason we got in trouble when we were kids, say returning home late for dinner.

"I told you we were eating at 6 o'clock," our mother said. "Where were you? Why weren't you looking at your watch?"

At first we may have been watching the time, but the game or the activity got so involving that we lost track of space and time. We were functioning in the moment. And one moment led to another.

Cooperative play is a means of getting people who have to work together on a regular basis more connected with each other. Unspoken resentments fade away. Office politics subside. As people begin to play and revert to a childlike innocence, they reveal wonderful things about themselves in the way they play. Too often people go to work believing they have to hide some of their goodwill because it will be used against them. So, many of us create these false "adult" selves, believing that we will need them to protect us from harm. In fact, embracing this attitude just keeps us from being the most authentic person we can be. We cheat ourselves and we cheat the company. That's because the childlike part of us, our "neotenous" self, is creative, joyful, and wise.

Early in my program I offer several guarantees. I tell everyone that they will have a good time—even if they don't want to! But I also tell them up front that they will learn interesting things that they didn't know about the people they are about to play with, and that these will be good things. Greek philosopher Plato, thousands of years ago wrote, "You can learn more about a person in an hour of play than in a year of conversation." Obviously I agree.

I also agree with a sign I always take note of when I walk past a shop on a section of Melrose Avenue in Los Angeles. It is right in the window of *The Wound-Up Toy Store* and is a quote by playwright George Bernard Shaw.

> "People don't stop playing because they grow old. They grow old because they stop playing."

Well *I've* never stopped playing and I know it has its roots way back in my childhood. Allow me to explain.

PART TWO

"PETER PAN" BEGINS TO FLY

CHAPTER 11

PLAY—THE EARLY YEARS

"Play gives children a chance to practice what they're learning."
—Mr. Rogers, Television Host (1928-2003)

My mother always called me "Peter Pan." She thought that I never wanted to grow up. Well she was partially correct. It's always been very important to me to retain all of the energy of that inner child of mine. It provides me a wondrous way of looking at the world. That attitude and my take on relationships have helped me forge the career path I have chosen for myself. Though I used to take umbrage when she used that Peter Pan label on me, lately I've come to see it as a supreme compliment. Thanks Mom!

When I was a kid the thing I liked to do more than anything else was play. I would spend hours with my friends participating in games like "Red Light, Green Light," "Ring-a-levio," "Giant Steps," and "Hide and Seek." What I didn't know then, but know for sure now, is that the play world is a child's natural way for personal growth and positive learning. As children we had a perfect medium, because games constantly involved us in the process of acting and feeling, reacting and experiencing.

As a small child I remember spending a lot of time alone. I seemed to be able to amuse myself very well. My favorite plaything was a set of wooden blocks. I would sit on the floor with the different shaped blocks strewn around me and build all kinds of fortresses and castles. Once I was satisfied with what I had created I liked to walk down the long hall which led from the front door of the apartment that we lived in, take one of my toy cars, and send it careening into the buildings I had just created. If I had to name that game today I would probably call it, "Construction 'n' Destruction."

Outside, when playing with the neighborhood kids, one of my favorite ball games was "Spud." Perhaps you played it too, but under a different name. In this game everyone was given a number from 1 to however many participants there were. One of us then became the ball bouncer. He or she would bounce the ball on the cement as hard as possible so it flew way up into the air. Then every kid would start running away from the center of activity. At the same moment the ball bouncer would yell out a number. Whoever's number it was had to return to the starting point and catch or retrieve the ball. Once they had complete possession they would holler, "Spud," which was the command for all the fleeting bodies to freeze in place. The person with the ball would now choose someone close to them to throw the ball at. If they hit the selected person, that person was given an "S" (for SPUD), and became the possessor of the ball in the next round. If "ball thrower" missed, he would be assigned the "S" and have to bounce the ball again. If you accumulated S.P.U.D. you were out of the game. The victor was the person still playing when everyone else was eliminated. The game required an ability to run fast and accuracy in throwing the ball and hitting someone. I especially liked the game because I was fleet of foot and my hand/eye coordination was very good. And isn't it true that we most enjoy what we do well?

One game, however, that I wasn't good at during my early days was softball. I was scared of the ball and usually dropped it when it was thrown to or hit at me. I developed the reputation of an individual who shouldn't be a top selection for any team. I vividly recall one day when I was about eight or nine that the two kids on the block who were considered the best ballplayers were acting as captains and choosing sides. Well Captain #1 picked his first choice and then Captain #2 picked his first choice. Again and again the two captains made selections. As usual no one was picking me. Finally I was the last one remaining and the two captains proceeded to argue over who would get me.

"He lost the game for us yesterday," shouted the captain who was to choose next. "I don't want him."

"Well I don't want him either," yelled the other captain. "He's no good!"

Is it any wonder that when I conduct my cooperative games seminar no one is left out, that everyone gets to play, and that I have developed ways to organize teams and groups so that everyone immediately feels included?

One of my all-time favorite games, which I still play with adults if the training facility is large enough, is known as "Red Light, Green Light." In this game there is a leader who takes on the role of the traffic cop. All other participants stand behind a line several yards away (30-40 yards is ideal). The traffic cop says, "Green Light" and then turns his back on the group. Everyone is allowed to advance as far as they dare. At some point the traffic cop yells, "Red Light" and spins around. The players must freeze in place. However if they are still moving they are sent back to the starting line, usually over their protests that they weren't moving. As in real life, the traffic cop prevails.

Once again the cop says, "Green Light" and turns his back again. People try to advance some more, or in the case of the ones sent all the way back, to gain back some of the ground they lost. Participants have options—they can advance just a few short steps and freeze so they protect themselves from getting caught, or make a mad dash forward trying to accumulate as many yards as they can. For the object of the game is to be the first to tag the traffic cop before he orders "Red Light" and turns around again. The one who gets there first has won, becomes the new Traffic Cop and the game begins anew.

This is the all-time perfect game in which to cheat. One technique, if you have been sent back to the starting line, is to use other people's bodies (that may be blocking the sight lines of the traffic cop) to slowly sneak up while the traffic cop is identifying other people who he saw moving when he turned around. Or you can fall to the floor just as you hear the command "Red Light." The traffic cop sees you frozen on the floor but usually is too preoccupied with others as you get up. And you're conveniently grabbing a few extra feet as you get into a standing position. I believe this game wouldn't be as much fun if you couldn't cheat.

To me it's like the opportunity I take as a grown up, when it's very late at night and I've checked that there are no cars coming in any direction, to sometimes go through the red light. Come on I'm sure you've done it too! Didn't someone once say "laws and rules are made to be broken?" Playing sometimes gives us a chance to practice that.

CHAPTER 12

PARDON ME BUT AREN'T YOU…?

"The secret of genius is to carry the spirit of childhood into maturity."
—*Thomas Huxley, Biologist (1825-1895)*

It's spring 1993 and my pal Steve Kohn, who at the time was selling corporate sponsorships in Los Angeles, has a business meeting with the advertising folks at a major grocery company. He invites me to come along as his "silent assistant." He feels I will have an opportunity to see him make the kind of presentation I'm going to have to perfect in order to sell my new team-building and stress-management LET'S PLAY AGAIN seminar.

We go to the corporate headquarters, arriving about 45 minutes before the scheduled appointment time. The reception room is filled to capacity so Steve suggests we visit a restaurant next door and have a soft drink. A half hour later we decide to head back. As Steve pays the cashier I wait for him near the entrance. There is a tall fellow, smiling broadly, approaching me. His look says "I know you" but I don't recognize him. He is now standing almost face-to-face as he inquires:

"Pardon me but aren't you Howie Papush?"

This is a dead giveaway. Only people who have known me for a very long time still refer to me as "Howie."

"Yes. Do I know you?" I ask.

"You sure do!"

Still not recognizing him, I say, "Am I going to be embarrassed when you tell me who you are?"

"Probably"— a pause, and then he declares, "I'm Owen Reilly."

"Owen Reilly! What are you doing in California? And how did you recognize me?"

Owen Reilly had been a childhood playmate who had lived with his family in the same apartment house I grew up in back in Flushing, New York. I hadn't seen him for many years. As a young boy I had adored his mother. She often acted as babysitter for my older brother and me when my parents went to weddings and other adult family events. In fact, when I was four or five, I told my mother one day that I wanted to be called "Steve Reilly" rather than by my own given name. That's how connected I felt to the Reilly family.

Now after all these years, here was a grownup Owen Reilly, greeting me in a restaurant in California, far from our hometown. Unbeknownst to me, he had lived in Los Angeles for several years; he was a computer consultant who also had a meeting with the grocery concern on that particular day, and he too had arrived early and decided to have a cool drink next door.

It seemed like a coincidence at that moment, but I have since learned that there are no coincidences. This was *meant* to happen because he had something important to share with me.

He asked if I was still working in television. He told me he had known about my job at *The Tonight Show*, but hadn't seen my production credit for a long time. I explained the decision I had made to leave that industry to become a motivational speaker. Then I started to tell him about LET'S PLAY AGAIN, and how I facilitated workshops for stressed business executives, using "cooperative games" and activities.

As I talked he began to smile and then to laugh. Believing that his reaction meant that he found my career a "trivial pursuit" (pun intended), I explained quite defensively that I was very serious about what I did, and saw great value in my seminars.

"That's not why I'm laughing," he interjected. "Don't you remember?"

"Remember what?" I asked.

"That's what you did when we were kids. You were *always*

organizing everybody in the neighborhood to play. You were our neighborhood version of the *Love Boat* Social Director!"

Wham—in a rush it all came flooding back to me. Yes, I *had* done that. Yes, long ago as a youngster—getting the other kids together to play "Punch Ball," "Giant Steps," or "Hide and Seek." Now I remembered!

Somehow I knew then that if the kids in the neighborhood were playing together, they wouldn't be teasing, or fighting with each other. I had intuitively realized even as a child that the right type of play brought individuals together. And now I was making a career out of this natural instinct I had had as a 10-year-old.

Finally I understood what was behind the "thunderbolt" I had experienced in the NBC Studios back in 1978 (I told you about it in the Prologue) while we were taping the television pilot. That night I knew the "play" segment with the principals in the show and the guest celebrities was meaningful to me in some way, but I didn't know exactly why. Now it all connected. It had seemed familiar because it reached back into my childhood and it had been talking to me. And years later I had finally acted on those instincts and created LET'S PLAY AGAIN.

CHAPTER 13

WHO'S AFRAID OF BIG, BAD BILL?

"Childhood is that wonderful time when all you have to do to lose weight is take a bath."
—*Joe Moore, Hawaiian Newscaster*

Owen Reilly was right in branding me our neighborhood's *Love Boat* Social Director. Somewhere around the age of 10 I started exhibiting leadership qualities and soon all the kids in the building where we lived began to depend on me to organize the group activities.

One of our favorite pastimes was a version of "punch ball" that we played in an area we called the "alleys" on Lawrence Street in Flushing where we lived. The alleys were actually a series of courtyards that ran the length of the back of the apartment building. The rules of the game were the same as for baseball—each team got three outs and the game was nine innings long. You made an out by "popping the ball up" to a fielder, or striking out by swinging and missing at three pitches. If a ground ball was fielded and thrown to the first baseman before the hitter got there you were out as well. You could hit singles, doubles, and triples. But every batter wished for a homerun, which was hard to do.

At the end of our narrow field was another even narrower alley. If you hit the ball into that alleyway on a fly you had your homerun. But the opposing team always positioned one of their best and largest players in front of the alley tunnel to catch or block any ball heading that way.

During the summers there were usually several punch ball games played in the course of a day. And, as Owen had reminded me, I organized just about all of them. Some actually went the full nine innings but that was never a given.

You see we had this surly superintendent named Bill who managed and maintained the building. Sometimes an apartment renter whose dwelling looked down on our "field of dreams" would call Bill to complain that the kids were making too much noise in the alley. Then Bill, the enforcer, would spring into action and break up our game and our fun. Because of this we were always on alert that Bill might show up.

But Bill did not *just* show up! He usually was in full charge, looking like a bull racing towards a matador's cape. It was a very scary picture. What made Bill ever so menacing was that he looked exactly like "Nikita Khrushchev." You know the Premier of Communist Russia, our country's bitter enemy during the 1950s when I was growing up. He was the man who once, during a speech at the United Nations, threatened to "bury" the United States. Well "our Khrushchev look-alike" was trying to get us too. He even tried to scare us into believing that the fun punch ball games could cause our families to be evicted from the building.

I usually took it upon myself to be the courageous one in the group. Yes, the sight of the charging superintendent Bill was scary, and at first I did head for the tunnel at the end of the courtyard and safety like everyone else. But after awhile I got wise to his antics, figuring he didn't have the right to grab or hurt us. At some point in my run I would stop and look defiantly at him—of course from a safe distance. He did not like that at all! He wanted us to fear him and he thought I was being disrespectful. But as the months passed, this game of cat and mice changed. I think Bill started to respect the pipsqueak kid Howie for standing up to him and not being totally frightened by his menacing demeanor. He never said anything directly to me but I could tell. Once in a while I even got a knowing smile from him.

Sometimes we even became brazen. You see, there was another courtyard that ran right alongside Bill's basement apartment. When we were sure that he was away from the building we would play right there in front of his windows. It was like flaunting our game in his face, though of course he wasn't home. The child's defiant "right to play."

But when he would come home and catch us in the act he'd get particularly angry and revert to his chasing ways. However, it was always worth it to me. Those punch ball games and our private war with the Nikita Khrushchev look-alike will always be a joyful, wonderful memory from my childhood.

CHAPTER 14

THE JOYS OF STICKBALL

> "People ask me what I do in winter when there's no baseball. I'll tell you what I do. I stare out the window and wait for spring."
> —Rogers Hornsby, Baseball Legend (1896-1963)

By the time I turned 12 my attention and focus turned away from punch ball to games of "stick ball." We played on the driveway of an automobile repair shop directly across the street from the apartment house where I lived. I would pair off with a neighborhood boy or a visiting cousin in a game filled with its own sense of drama and danger. One fellow would be up at bat, standing beside a rectangular box that had been drawn on the garage door. The other would pitch a rubber ball or a tennis ball overhand to him. If the pitcher threw the ball and the batter swung and missed, it was a strike. If the batter didn't swing but the ball struck the door within the box, that too was a strike. Once again it was three outs and then the pitcher and batter switched roles. There was no running to bases in this game. It was just pitching and batting. Let me tell you more about the ground rules because they are very important to this story.

    If the batter hit the ball on the ground and it was fielded by the pitcher cleanly, pitcher suddenly became an infielder and had to make an imaginary throw towards first base. That counted as an out. A ball hit past the pitcher though was a single; a ball hit hard enough to make it across the street and strike our building was a double. If the ball was hit far and deep so that it struck the facade higher than the third floor of our four-story building, you had a triple. And any ball hit onto the roof was an automatic homerun. Usually the batter would broadcast the flight of the ball as it headed towards the roof. I have to tell you a homerun was a very exciting event in our stickball game!

There could be major complications, though. You see our apartment building wall was lined with neighbors' windows. The game was safe if the soft rubber ball we used just hit the brick wall, but if it struck somebody's window we held our breath! And if it broke the window we ran! We ran of course because it was important to get out of there before a neighbor got to their smashed window and looked out to see who the culprits were. Bill, our menacing super, would then have the goods on us and of course it would be reported to our parents, who would be charged for the damage.

But we couldn't resist playing our stickball game right there. At the time there was no little league field or park close enough to go to. We played in the streets and we took our risks. It really was great fun. And it was a rite of passage too. Here we were kids growing up in a city that featured three beloved major league teams. These games of stickball were fantasy versions of the Giants vs. the Yankees or the Giants vs. the Dodgers. I was always the Giants because I idolized Willie Mays. We planned our lineups and announced the game as it went along. Whenever I came to bat as Willie I knew I had to do well. I felt I owed it to him!

Many years later, when my nephew Gregg was a teenager he and his dad, mom, and sister Michele came to visit me in California. We started to exchange stories about our forms of play when we were kids and I discovered he was a big stickball fan too. I told him about my fun experiences so long ago. Gregg immediately challenged me to a game. Though I had not played in many years and was 23 years his senior I felt that I could still give him some good competition, perhaps even win. We bought a broom from a hardware store, cut off the brush part, scoped out a handball court on a school playground in my neighborhood, used chalk to draw a square box on the wall, and began to play. The game ended abruptly with Gregg winning decisively and me reeling from the sorest shoulder pain I can ever remember. It was clear then and it is clear now that my stickball-playing days are over.

But late at night, in my dreams, I sometimes return to Flushing and those great games of yesteryear. I am still Willie Mays up at bat and I just know that I am about to hit the ball up on the roof of my old apartment house for a homerun!

CHAPTER 15

ONE "PENNY" THAT'S WORTH A FORTUNE

"The best and most beautiful things in the world cannot be seen or even touched. They must be felt with the heart."
—Helen Keller, American Educator (1880-1968)

Memories of the people who inhabited my life during my growing up days are hard to come by. As I've recounted, I remember Superintendent Bill and the Reilly family, but most of the other kids and their parents have faded from my memory. Through the years, though, there was *one* other person I recalled fondly. Her name was Penny, she was one of my mother's best friends, and she lived with her husband Joe and their three children in our building.

About the time I turned 16 she and Joe bought a house in another part of our town and moved away. Many years passed but for some reason the memory of Penny always stayed with me. Was it because she had always been nice to me when I was a kid? Or was there some other reason she had stuck in my mind? Eventually I moved from New York to California to continue my television career, and memories of Flushing faded away even more.

When Owen Reilly came back into my life he organized a dinner party one night and reunited me with his sister Mary Ellen, who had also moved to California years before. That evening we exchanged stories about the "old days" and some of our neighbors. I was amazed at how much they remembered about the kids and their parents, and how little I could recall. At one point Mary Ellen brought up the name of Penny's daughter Marcia, whom she had been good friends with when we were kids.

"Did you ever stay in touch with her?" I inquired.

"Sure," Mary Ellen replied.

"Did you ever get the chance to visit her when you were back in New York?"

"No, but I have seen her out here in California. She moved down to San Diego years ago."

"She did?" I was surprised. "I often think of her Mom, Penny, and wonder if she's still alive."

"She sure is," Mary Ellen responded. "In fact she also lives out here, not too far from Marcia, in Chula Vista. I saw her not too long ago when I was visiting at Marcia's house."

I was amazed. Penny was living in California a couple of hours from me and I had never known it! Instantly I felt I needed to contact her. Mary Ellen supplied me with Penny's telephone number and, excitedly, I called the next day.

"Hi," was the greeting after the phone had rung a few times. The voice sounded very youthful, which was a little surprising because I knew Penny had to be close in age to my mother, who was then almost 80.

"Is this Penny?" I inquired.

"Yes and who is *this*?" Her response was playful.

"This is someone you haven't spoken to in many years," I said.

"Well talk some more! Your voice sounds familiar."

"Oh I don't think so. You see Penny we haven't spoken in years, since I was a teenager and lived in Flushing."

"Who *is* this?"

I could tell she was quite curious.

"This is Howard Papush."

"Oh, Howie. What a wonderful surprise."

Excitedly I told her how much I had thought about her through the years; how I had just visited with Owen and Mary Ellen and had learned that she was living here in California. She, too, seemed excited about the phone call. Before we went much further I said, "Penny, I want to come see you, perhaps even this weekend. Would you have time for a visit? Her response: "What do you like to eat? I'll fix you anything you want!"

And so that weekend I drove down to Chula Vista and my reunion with long-lost Penny. And what a reunion it was! I learned so many things from her about my childhood. She remembered me so well as a baby and as a little boy growing up in the neighborhood. She was not surprised at all to learn about my motivational speaking programs. She recalled my innate organizing ability with the neighborhood kids. And then she told me something that had been key to my growing up experience with her.

"Don't you remember when I used to play Super Girl with you? I used to tie a kitchen towel around my neck, stand on a chair and then jump off, pretending I was flying, and tell you I was Super Girl. You would watch me with your eyes wide and just laugh and laugh."

Now I was beginning to understand why the memory of Penny had always been so important to me. She, unlike the adults around me—my mother and father—had been the one to teach me about fun and to show me that adults had imaginations and liked to play too. I wanted more information and Penny, who still has a good memory, began to tell me other stories of our time together when I was a kid.

I spent several hours at her house that day. She fed me much too much food and told me all about her life. Her husband Joe had become ill right around the time they decided to move to California to be close to Marcia and her husband and their granddaughter. He died two years after they arrived. To deal with the sadness of his passing she became a teaching assistant at a local school. She works with handicapped kids and, for the past 23 years, evryone has known her as Grandma Penny.

In fact in 2003 she was named San Diego's "Volunteer of the Year." She is still dispensing the love and caring that she provided for a little boy growing up in Flushing, Queens so many years before.

Our relationship has endured. Now 10 years after our reunion in Chula Vista I talk to Penny by phone regularly and every once in a while go down to San Diego to see her. She's 89 and I still marvel at her energy, her spunk, and most of all her playfulness. Whenever I'm with her I experience such joy.

For most people a penny may not be that important. For me this Penny is one of the most valuable presents I have ever received!

PART THREE

IS THIS TV OR AM I IN A SANDBOX?

CHAPTER 16

SUPER GUIDE CONDUCTS THE NBC TOUR

> "Begin doing what you want to do now. We are not living in eternity. We have only this moment, sparkling like a star in our hand—and melting like a snowflake."
>
> —*Sir Francis Bacon, English Philosopher (1561-1626)*

Fresh out of college, where I majored in speech and broadcasting, and finished with my active duty military service obligation, I began my journey into the television industry. I knew that I wanted to be a television producer someday, so headed to the networks in Manhattan to see what entry level jobs might be available. At NBC I learned that there was a policy of hiring from within. Promising candidates started in the mailroom or as members of the Guest Relations staff, and moved into production and technical jobs as positions opened up.

I chose to interview with Guest Relations. I was glib and personable and the manager of the department seemed to like that. He explained there were two options available: either to be a "page," who ushered at the various TV shows shot at the studios in Rockefeller Center, or a "tour guide." In making a final decision he wanted to know if I was "good with kids." Slam dunk!

And so I was hired to be a tour guide, welcoming the sightseers and the many school groups that came through the facilities eager to get a behind-the-scenes look at the television studios, and perhaps catch a view of a celebrity or two.

Being a successful tour guide required a few special abilities. Besides having to master the many informational facts and figures for the various stops through the studios, you needed to be able to walk backwards gracefully as you gestured from one highlight to another.

"Here on your left is Studio 3. This is the home of the TV soap opera, *The Doctors*. The show first went on the air in 1963. It is shown every day on NBC at 2:30. Perhaps you can get a glimpse of James Pritchett who plays the part of Dr. Matt Powers..."

We tour guides felt we had the prestige Guest Relations position. As we viewed it, the pages were just glorified ushers who stood in the main lobby of NBC making sure that the ticket lines were orderly, and then seated the audiences. We on the other hand were teachers and communicators. I liked that.

Some of us were even thought of as "super guides" for our special affinity with the adults and youngsters. This may sound immodest but I was one of them. People enjoyed my tours and I made sure they were memorable.

At one of the stops the group was led into an historic radio studio. Then the guide entered a sealed sound effects room and demonstrated the various objects that had been used to make the specialized sounds listeners heard during the heyday of radio. Coconut shells rapped on a wood board became the sound of horse's hoofs. Crinkling cellophane created the sound of fire, and so forth. For the grand finale we turned the lights off in the studio so it was pitch black, and reenacted a dramatic scene. Each of the tour guides was responsible for creating their own script. We had fun doing it and, judging from the tours' response, they enjoyed the results.

During my days as a tour guide I witnessed some behavior patterns on the part of the staff that bothered me a lot. Each of my fellow guides was aspiring to be something else. There were "wannabe" actors and actresses, "wannabe" TV producers and directors, programmers, and future executives. But for now we were all tour guides. Some of my colleagues were frustrated that career opportunities weren't happening fast enough and their frustration showed up in very negative ways. I remember having a few serious conversations with colleagues giving them my "take" on the importance of being a professional—which meant showing the tourists a good time—even as we longed to be somewhere else. I remember suggesting they make their work "play" so that they could continue to make the four or five tours they led each day fresh and new and fun even to them.

Then one day one of my colleagues, Rick Rosner, announced that he had just gotten a job with *Candid Camera* and was leaving the staff. To say I was envious would be putting it mildly. That had always been one of my favorite TV shows and I had often fantasized how much fun it must be to work on that production. I wished him well and continued my search for an entry level position somewhere as Rick took on his new position. Often I imagined what great times Rick must be having. About three months later I happened to bump into him on the street as I left NBC for lunch.

"How's your job going?" I asked with great enthusiasm.

"What job? I've been searching for a few weeks now."

"But what about *Candid Camera*?"

"Oh I haven't worked there for weeks. They hire and fire all the time. That's not a fun place to be."

I was shocked. Here I had fantasized what a great time Rick was having at *Candid Camera,* and now I was learning that he was no longer there. As we talked I kept thinking to myself, "Well maybe they have a job open there and wouldn't it be neat if…"

Rick must have read my mind. "Listen they always have jobs open. This is their number. You should call them up."

The next day I called the number. I had my resumé and an envelope at the ready. All I needed to know was the name of the producer so I could address a cover letter to him. The switchboard operator connected me to someone in the producer's office. I requested the necessary information.

"Who are *you*?" she inquired. I gave her my name, explained that I was looking for a production assistant's job with the show and wanted to send my resumé to the appropriate person. She put me on hold. After a few moments she was back on the line. "Our producer is Bob Shanks. He wants to know if you can come in and see him tomorrow."

The producer wanted to see me even before I sent him my resumé? This was good news. We made an appointment for the following day at 2:00 pm. And for the next 24 hours I imagined how much fun it would be, if I was just lucky enough to get a job with that classic show. Boy was I in for a surprise!

CHAPTER 17

A CANDID LOOK AT "CANDID CAMERA"

"In the middle of difficulty lies opportunity."
—*Albert Einstein, German-American Physicist (1879-1955)*

Have you ever had an interview for a job and knew you were the perfect person for the position? Well, that's the way it played out the next day in Bob Shanks' office. We created a rapport immediately and he seemed to be impressed with my college background and my attitude. He was quite candid (pun intended) about the position, noting that it was the lowest job on the rung, and that everyone made excessive demands on production assistants. He explained the duties and the potential pitfalls. He even went so far as to talk about specific members of the crew and how difficult they could be.

It did not faze me. I told him that I had been on active duty in the Army less than a year before, had drawn my share of distasteful KP duties, and had coped with the demands of surly sergeants. I said that I was up for the challenge and sensed he was about to offer me my first "dream job." But then I confessed that I did not have a driver's license (part of the job description) and his face fell. He explained that it was a key element and that he couldn't possibly hire me if I didn't drive. The truth is I had a learner's permit but, because I didn't have a car of my own, had never gotten around to taking the driving test.

Realizing that I wasn't going to get the position, I said, "Bob I would really do well in this job. I am going to get my license as fast as I can and then you're going to hear from me. Maybe there will be another job available."

I set out immediately to finally learn how to drive. Was I motivated! I can still recall the driving lessons with my father and how I pushed him to teach me everything I needed to know to pass my test. Within weeks I made an appointment with the Department of Motor Vehicles and secured my license on the first try. The very next day I called Bob Shanks again. I reminded his secretary who I was and told her to tell him that I now had my license and was ready to go. Guest what? Within days a production assistant's job miraculously opened up again and I got it.

The first few weeks working for the show were challenging and exhilarating. As Bob had initially warned me, some of the location crew were particularly demanding. Besides being the designated driver, the job involved going for coffee, handling the crew's timesheets, helping with the setup, and securing "releases" from anyone filmed on location.

Another of my responsibilities I liked very, very much. From time to time I would be asked to take part as an "extra" in one of the scenes being filmed. Sometimes I even had lines to say, most of them improvised. It was great fun and a wonderful source of "play." One night we filmed at the legendary Stork Club, then the "in place" for important and influential New Yorkers. The shoot was designed to reveal what might happen if some of the regular patrons were refused the star treatment they were used to when they arrived at the nightclub.

Let me set the scene. A velvet rope barred the entrance to the main room and one of our staff "acted" as the maitre d'. When a "regular" arrived he was told that he had to wait behind the rope until his reservation could be honored, and that might take awhile. In the meantime we "fake" customers would stroll in, state our names, and be seated without hesitation! The hidden camera remained fixed on the faces of those regulars who had been denied immediate access. You could see their frustration and rising anger. That night I probably said, "Papush, table for two," thirty times. And each time I was seated immediately, much to the consternation of the folks stranded behind the rope.

Then there was the time we set up at a large supermarket in New Jersey. The premise was that the store was about to honor the one-millionth customer to pass through the checkout counters. Attractively gift-wrapped packages filled a shopping cart prominently displayed at the front of the store. Several of us, acting as customers, formed a line at one of the checkout counters and waited for an unsuspecting "target" to get in line. Once that occurred, another *Candid Camera* staff member got in line behind that person. Soon one of our lead actors arrived, introduced himself as manager of the store, and began counting, "997, 998, 999."

Pointing to our unsuspecting shopper, he said, "Congratulations. You're about to become the one-millionth customer to have your groceries rung up since the store first opened a few years ago. As you go through the check-out line, we're going to make an announcement on the public address system, have a photographer from the local newspaper take your picture, and then we will present you with several valuable gifts."

Of course, all of our "pigeons" that day were thrilled. They'd claim that they had never won anything before. As the line moved forward they would be anticipating their moment in the sun. The *Candid Camera* troop now would go into action. I, who was standing in line in front of our subject, would start mumbling aloud, "Now let's see. I have milk, orange juice, bread—oh I forgot to get eggs."

Then I would leave the line and disappear. Now the person standing behind our unsuspecting guy (also a *Candid Camera* staff member) would begin to inquire about what the store manager had said. Our subject would explain that he was about to become the millionth customer. Our staff member would ask how that could be since someone had just left the line.

People, in their desire to retain the millionth-customer designation, might then offer to have the person behind them step ahead so that once again he or she would be number 1,000,000. This was my cue to come back and insist on getting in my old place in line. Some of our unsuspecting "marks," seeing me as a threat to their prize, would offer to pay for my groceries if I didn't get back in line.

The longer we did the "bit" that day the wilder it became. It was straight out of a Marx Brothers movie. To see unsuspecting individuals act in such bizarre ways up-close was fascinating.

But the weirdness was haunting the *Candid Camera* offices as well. One day, after returning from a shoot, I sat down at an unoccupied desk in the main office area and was busy making out the crew's timesheets. Lots of loud, raucous noise was coming from inside the office of Allen Funt, creator and executive producer of the show. I imagined he might be watching some of the recent footage and enjoying what he was seeing. Suddenly I noticed that everyone in the vicinity had left their desks and vanished. At almost the same moment Bob Schwartz, one of the location producers, approached me and said, "You don't look comfortable there. Get up and follow me and I'll find another place for you to sit."

I told him that I felt just fine at that desk but he was insistent. So I followed him down a corridor to the writer's area, where he motioned me to an empty office, and told me to do my work in there. When he left he closed the door behind him. "Why was he putting me in a writer's office?" I pondered. But because I was the "new kid on the block" I just followed orders. Eventually I finished my work, opened the door, and discovered that it was past 7:00 p.m. and everyone had left.

The next day, back out on location, I asked Bob why he had stuck me away in a closed office. It was then that I learned what had been going on. The boss, Mr. Funt, had not been enjoying the footage he had been viewing at all. In fact he was very angry and felt that it had been a wasted day of shooting, and wasted money. Eventually he had burst out of his office looking to pick a fight with anyone in his line of vision so that he could fire that person. It was his regular routine and the staff had witnessed it many times. So whenever they heard angry sounds coming from the boss's office, it was time to "become scarce." They found hiding places or simply left until he calmed down. Bob liked my work and had chosen to save me.

But that was only the beginning. Soon I learned a variety of things about the working conditions at this, my first job in the television industry. Morale was poor. There was no sense of teamwork here. Everyone was in it for themselves, and some had sharp knives ready for their co-workers.

Producer Shanks' appendix burst shortly after I started working there and he had to have emergency surgery. While he was on sick leave, two of the key associates (one of them known as the "Dragon Lady") convinced Funt that the show could get along fine without Shanks. So the nicest and most professional guy in the office was fired even before he could return to work!

Also, everyone loved to gossip about each other, and they usually found awful things to say. Quickly I realized that this wasn't a fun community at all. But I endured it because I was learning a lot about film shoots and I knew that this could help me in my career.

Then one day, a mere two months into the job, I was fired too! Funt felt the budget was too high and that the staff should be cut. So they started with me, the guy who was getting $80 a week! Now I remembered what Rick Rosner had told me months before about his experience at *Candid Camera*. "That's not a fun place to be. They hire and fire all the time."

I knew I needed another job fast, hopefully one with a group of people who were going to be much nicer to work with. Little did I know that I was about to go from Hell to Heaven.

CHAPTER 18

WELCOME TO THE FUN HOUSE

"Pleasure in the job puts perfection in the work."
—Aristotle, Greek Philosopher (384-322 B.C.)

A friend of mine, hearing of my firing, encouraged me to call an old childhood friend of hers, Ben Joelson, who was a successful TV producer. Ironically, he had once worked at *Candid Camera* too, and she thought he would be sympathetic to the experience I had just been through—as well as a good contact. Ben was now developing game shows with his partner Art Baer and said on the phone he would be willing to meet with me, though no jobs were immediately open.

The reception area over at the Baer-Joelson offices in the Buckingham Hotel in mid-Manhattan was incredibly calm compared to the dark *Candid Camera* atmosphere I had just left. The friendly receptionist quickly ushered me into Art and Ben's private office and I was warmly welcomed by two smiling guys, sitting side by side behind matching desks. Our initial conversation was about Allen Funt and the troubled time I had just come from. It was easy to talk with them.

Early into our chat Art began to toss a squashed piece of paper towards a miniature basketball hoop across the room.

"How much do you want to bet I can make three shots in a row?" he asked me playfully. Before I had time to answer, shot #1 had swished through the hoop.

"Well I'm not going to bet against someone who has the power to hire me."

"Good answer," Ben responded as Art's second shot matched his first.

"Okay you try," Art said, handing me the third wad of paper.

Now I can't recall if I made the first basket or not. But I do remember that little kid's voice in my head saying loudly, "These guys are fun! They like to play! This is exactly where you want to be."

Art and Ben explained they were developing a game show, which they were calling, *Fractured Phrases*. Ben handed me a card and asked me to read aloud what was on it. Printed were the words, DEAF ANTHEM STIR HIKES SAIGON. I started to read the words to myself.

"No read them out loud. It's a famous saying," Art directed.

"Deaf anthem stir hikes Saigon," I said aloud.

"Stress different words and syllables and you'll get it," Ben coached.

"Deaf *anthem* stir hikes Saigon," I offered.

"Great. You're saying it," Art enthused.

"What am I saying?" I still had no clue. "Deaf anthem *stir* hikes Saigon," I tried. "*Deaf* anthem stir hikes Saigon. Deaf anthem stir hikes *Saigon*." I had no idea what the famous saying was. Finally Art and Ben told me.

"It's '*The phantom strikes again.*' Don't you hear it? deafanthemstirhikessaigon. If you run it together you hear it."

Now they handed me another card. On it was written HITS SUP HERD HITS SUP LANE HITS SUE BERMAN. "Try this one out," they said.

"Hits sup herd hits sup lane hits sue *berman*," was my first take. "*Hits* sup herd hits sup lane hits sue berman. It's sup herd *it's a plane it's* sue berman." Now I was into it. "It's a bird, it's a plane, it's *Sue Berman*."

Art and Ben were laughing hysterically. Finally the light bulb went off in my head. "It's a bird, it's a plane, it's *Superman*." I had finally gotten it.

"So that's the show we're working on," Art explained. "We have a run-through with NBC in a few weeks. If we sell it to them we're going to have to add a lot of people to the staff. So we'll hold onto your resumé and see what happens."

I left their office very enthused. I really liked them and I hoped something would happen and that there would be a job for me. A few weeks later, as I continued my search for work, I got a call from that friendly Baer/Joelson receptionist. The show had just sold and they wanted me to come in for an official interview. Boy was I excited!

This time I was introduced to Stu Billett, who was going to be line producer for the series. (Years later he would team up with Ralph Edwards to develop and produce the incredibly successful *The People's Court*.) Our talk went well. Though he was not as playful as Art and Ben, he was very animated and had great enthusiasm for the new project, and I liked him. He must have liked me too because a couple of days later he called to offer me a job.

What a revelation! The Baer/Joelson office was one big fun house. People were friendly. Art and Ben constantly bought lunch for everyone. Several times a day Art challenged me to his office basketball or office baseball games, which of course he always won. It was like being on a playground. As the staff got to know each other better we developed into a loving family. In fact, on the weekends, I missed not being at the Buckingham Hotel.

Each Monday we welcomed one another back with warm hugs. People were always bringing food to the office to share with co-workers. We put together what we thought was a terrific show. Everything was done in a fun, relaxed but efficient mode. Here was a good model for a working experience. People could come to work, have fun, and still do their jobs well. I decided that the *Candid Camera* experience had been just an anomaly.

Unfortunately our "happy home" didn't last. The ratings for the show started off low, remained low, and after 13 weeks we were cancelled. Sadly, Art and Ben had to dismantle the staff. Fortunately other interesting jobs came along. But in all those early working years, I could never find the kind of playful and loving atmosphere that I had experienced with Art and Ben. My association with them was to be renewed years later, but until we were reunited I had several tough situations to endure.

There was the production work at WNBC-TV in New York for

fseveral years where I finally got my first producing credit. I met a wonderful woman there, Raysa Bonow, who is still a friend to this day. She was lots of fun and made my days tolerable, but when she left, and the politics and infighting at the station became too much, I left too. Next I developed, produced, and directed a syndicated arts and crafts show. Once all the episodes were shot I traveled across the country, trying to convince station managers to buy our project. It was a tough sell. Los Angeles was one of the last stops on the tour. I immediately fell in love with it. But that really was no surprise. As a kid growing up in New York I had always fantasized that one day I would be living in Los Angeles. A year later my wife and I decided to move there to further our careers.

And that's when I got the chance to hook up with Art and Ben again, though briefly. They had left for Hollywood years before to write for *The Carol Burnett Show*. Now their production company was active again and they were developing a new game show for ABC. When they learned I was living in L.A. they made me an offer—come and work for them on spec and help develop the show. If it sold they would be able to pay me well and give me a producer's credit. I jumped at the chance.

Once again we had a great time developing the show and we got a chance to play too, just like in the "old days." Art had even developed new office games to challenge me. Unfortunately ABC turned the concept down and I realized it was time to find a paying job. Reluctantly I had to say goodbye to them once again.

But new fortune smiled upon me. Years before, while I was working for WNBC-TV in New York, I had interviewed unsuccessfully for a production job with *The Tonight Show*. Now that they were on the West Coast I decided to try again with their new producer, Fred deCordova. I mailed my resumé and a "playful" note to him, and even before I had a chance to follow up, I got a call from associate producer Peter Lassally's secretary, wanting to schedule an interview.

At our meeting Peter and I connected easily. He was fun to talk to. We discussed our careers, our take on the television industry, and then at one point he said, "Fred and I aren't leaving so where do you think you'd fit in?"

"What about a talent coordinator's position?" I suggested. That job involved both booking talent for the show, and then interviewing and preparing questions that Johnny Carson could use during the guest's appearance. Peter wondered if I would be happy doing that. He was impressed with my previous public affairs programming credits and compared that to what he called "*The Tonight Show* fluff." I countered that I had always longed to work in the entertainment arena and felt my knowledge would carry over.

He was also concerned that I was overqualified for a talent coordinator's position since I had been a producer for several years. I countered that if I was indeed overqualified it would only make the show look better than it now was. It worked! The next day I was offered a job.

So in August of 1973 I began my tenure at *The Tonight Show*, and stayed for four years. There were good times and there were bad times. The show was not the fun place that working with Art and Ben had always been. But I created my own fun by getting the chance to give many talented folks their first exposure on national television—people such as Jay Leno, Arnold Schwarzenegger, Suzanne Somers, Sylvester Stallone, Natalie Cole, Marvin Hamlisch, Cheryl Ladd, Dr. Carl Sagan, and the outrageous Andy Kaufman. That is the subject for another book.

There are, however, some stories and situations that stand out during those *Tonight Show* days that I believe played a significant part in my becoming "Dr. Play." Let me share a few of them with you.

CHAPTER 19

JOHNNY CARSON LIKES TO PLAY

"I was so naïve as a kid I used to sneak behind the barn and do nothing."
—*Johnny Carson, Television Host (1925-present)*

When I first joined *The Tonight Show* Johnny Carson was quite frisky, and having lots of fun doing physical bits on the program. I watched him play tennis with Jimmy Connors, dive off a 20-foot-tower under the watchful eyes of a stuntman, repot garden plants with "drill sergeant" PBS horticulturist Thalassa Cruso, play with Joan Embry's San Diego Zoo animals, and even sample exotic food laced with bugs that made the studio audience turn squeamish.

Do you remember that classic moment when actor Ed Ames, who played "Mingo" on the TV show *Daniel Boone*, pitched axes with Johnny on the show? The outline of a gunslinger drawn on a wooden board was wheeled onstage. Ames took a position several yards away and threw first. Incredibly the ax landed exactly where the guy's two legs connected to the torso! The audience exploded in laughter. Ed quickly stepped forward to retrieve the ax but the "knowing" Johnny grabbed his arm before he could remove it. As the uproar died down Johnny uttered the famous line:

"A new program—Frontier Rabbi!"

This famous incident was shown on *The Tonight Show's* prime-time anniversary program for years afterward and is now one of the highlights of the "Ultimate Carson Collection" series of DVDs.

I, too, had the good fortune to develop a classic and

outrageous *Tonight Show* moment. I think of it as an early "Dr. Play happening." During the first few months of my *Tonight Show* career, a press agent called to say he had a perfect guest for the show. The subject's name was Hugh McDonald and he was a martial arts expert with a special talent in the use of swords and knives. Told that he was very personable, a terrific instructor, and someone Johnny could have a lot of fun with, I scheduled a meeting so that he could do a personal demonstration for me. Though McDonald turned out to be exactly who his agent said he would be, I still wasn't totally sold.

So McDonald provided the clincher. As a closing activity he would have Johnny lie prone on the floor with a large watermelon placed on his chest and stomach. Standing over Johnny, he would take his sharpest sword and cut the watermelon in half without penetrating any part of Johnny's body!

I was psyched. I could envision how this spot might play out. First the playful Johnny would try to duplicate Hugh's acrobatic moves but would screw up, eliciting lots of audience laughter. Then, when McDonald introduced his concluding feat, I could imagine Johnny feigning surprise and fear. Of course he would know in advance what was supposed to happen. He would reluctantly lie down. Our director would get great close-ups of Johnny making frightened faces. Then there would be the moment of impact—the watermelon splitting in half, and Johnny checking his body for wounds.

At the booking meeting the next morning I presented the proposed spot to the producers and other talent coordinators. Everyone listened attentively and then Fred suggested that I go directly to Johnny and try and sell it to him. This surprised me. Normally Fred acted as a shield for Johnny and was the one who brought him all of our ideas. But here he was telling me to seek an audience with our star and give him the details myself. I was both excited and scared. This was the first time I was going to speak with Johnny directly about a guest, and I wanted to make a really good pitch because I instinctively felt that the spot, if he would agree to it, could be a memorable one.

Johnny and I met the next day. He was friendly and seemed

interested in knowing what I wanted to discuss. I told him about my martial arts find, saving the "watermelon finale" for last. He thought for a few moments and then asked if I had checked out the guy. I told him that we had already met, that he was very personable, and that he had displayed his proficiency with the weapons for me. "If you think he's that good then let's do it," Johnny responded.

Three weeks later, exactly one week before Christmas Day 1973, my holiday present to America aired on national television. Hugh McDonald was a guest on *The Tonight Show* coast to coast. He leaped into the air with martial arts precision; he twirled his long-bladed swords; he instructed Johnny on the proper use of the weapons, which, as I predicted, Johnny playfully screwed up.

Then McDonald "proposed" the watermelon stunt. Johnny balked (following our unwritten script), finally allowing Hugh to "talk him into it," urged on by the audience's roar of applause and anticipation. "Reluctantly" he lay down on a mat. Hugh and his assistant gently placed the very large watermelon on Johnny's chest. Johnny mugged at how heavy it felt. Hugh did a few practice swings. Johnny displayed exaggerated looks of fear and trepidation for the cameras—which I'm sure had some reality to them. The audience, excited and nervous, laughed at every antic.

Finally McDonald lifted the sharp sword high over his head and thrust it down towards the prone body beneath him. The sword shot through the watermelon without a bit of resistance. The large fruit split in half, falling off Johnny's chest in opposite directions. The band played "ta-dah" as Johnny lay there, feeling his chest to make sure it was still intact, and searching for any gushing blood, but finding only watermelon juice on his shirt. A close-up showed that he had not been wounded. Producer deCordova turned to me along the sidelines, smiled broadly, and said, "That was *great!*"

Johnny was helped to his feet and appreciatively thanked Hugh for his expertise—and for not slicing him in half—while the audience applauded wildly. During the commercial break, once he had changed out of his juice-stained shirt, Johnny returned to his familiar desk and winked and nodded over at me, a sign of his pleasure with the success of the spot. As the "new kid" on the *Tonight*

Show staff I felt accepted for the first time since I had begun working there about four months before.

The next day, as I ate lunch in the NBC commissary, I heard people at a nearby table excitedly talking about "Johnny and the watermelon" bit. Several friends called me during the next few days asking whether I had been in the studio for the martial arts appearance, not realizing that I was the one who had brought it to the show. It was such a hit that for years later it occupied a position of honor on *The Tonight Show* Anniversary editions.

During my LET'S PLAY AGAIN seminars I *always* build in surprises and twists (no watermelons yet) that will make my audiences laugh and smile. I firmly believe that my days at *The Tonight Show*, watching the "master" at work, had a tremendous influence on the "entertainer" as well as educator I've now become. Thanks, Johnny!

CHAPTER 20

DON'T BE NERVOUS— YOU'RE GREGORY PECK!

"Feel the fear and do it anyway."
—Susan Jeffers, Self-help Author

During my time at *The Tonight Show* I had the chance to meet and work with many famous people. One of the most celebrated was Hollywood legend Gregory Peck. He was appearing on the show to promote his starring role in the film, *MacArthur*, and I was assigned to prepare his interview with Johnny. We had had a pleasant conversation on the phone a few days before; I took lots of notes and arranged a list of questions for Johnny to ask him during the visit.

On taping day Peck arrived at the studios all by himself. This surprised me—most stars of his stature usually traveled with entourages. After escorting him through the make-up process I took him to his dressing room and began to brief him on the questions Johnny might be asking. As we went over the material, I noticed his hands were shaking.

"Are you nervous?" I asked.

"Terribly!" was the instant reply in his noted stentorian voice.

"But you're Gregory Peck! How can you be nervous?"

"Give me a script, give me some lines, and I'll be Gregory Peck. But don't ask me to be myself. That's too uncomfortable for me."

In the past I had worked with other guests who were nervous before the show, but I was really surprised that a person of the stature of Gregory Peck would get so nervous as well. I acted to calm his fears. As I saw it, my job as a talent coordinator was not only to book a guest and then write an interview and the introduction for Johnny. I also wanted to "play" coach and prepare the guest so that he might "shine" on the show. And here was a major, major star feeling totally anxious.

I suggested this idea to him: surrender to the uncomfortable situation he found himself in, and choose to have fun with the interview. In the past I had noticed that the guests with the most impact played with the moment. So until it was his turn to take a seat next to Johnny I kept reminding him that his mission that night was to have fun, nothing else. Initially he seemed to relax, but as the time grew closer, I sensed he was getting nervous again

Our first guest that night was a juggler-comedian, who launched unique items into the air as he kept up a steady patter of funny lines and observations. He was very entertaining to the audience and to Johnny too. Now, during the commercial break, the once again shaking Gregory Peck and I waited behind the curtain backstage for him to be introduced. Suddenly I had a brainstorm! Heading straight for the juggler, who was packing up his props, I asked to borrow the three milk bottles he had just used in his act. Before he had time to decide, I seized them and was hurrying back to where Mr. Peck was standing.

"Take these," I declared, thrusting them into his arms. "When Johnny introduces you I want you to carry these bottles onto the stage. Then as the audience applause dies down, and before he can say anything, you say, 'Johnny for my first trick,' then pause, and see what happens."

Gregory Peck was looking at me in disbelief. But I held my ground. "You told me you needed a script, some lines in order to be Gregory Peck. Well here is your script. Trust me. Johnny will laugh, the audience will laugh, you'll be starting out with a sense of playfulness, some fun, and I know your fear will go away and you will be just fine." From the look in his eyes I knew that he wasn't sure this would work, but he seemed willing to try.

Johnny sized up the situation instantly, pointing to the milk bottles Peck carried on with him, knowing something was "up." He motioned Peck to his seat, and waited for the audience applause to die down. When the Academy Award®-winner uttered the lines from his "script," "Johnny, for my first trick…" our host broke into laughter and the audience went wild!

A few days later I received this note from Gregory Peck:

> Dear Howard,
> I have had more compliments on the
> Tonight Show appearance than on my
> last six movies. You were all helpful
> and generous, and I appreciated it.
> Thank you for the last minute
> inspiration about carrying on the bottles.
> It was the ice breaker I needed.
> All the best.
> Sincerely,
> Gregory Peck

As I look back to my days at *The Tonight Show* thirty years ago I realize more than ever that the philosophy and message I bring to corporate America today was being formed way back then.

Early in each seminar I talk about the choice individuals have every day at work. You can either choose the notion that you are going to "have fun" during the course of that day. Or you can be depressed and miserable. Yes you might have too much to do; yes you may be dealing with difficult co-workers, bosses and clients; yes you have to make tough decisions for the good of the company or your department.

But all of this can be done in a balanced way. You can stay in touch with your lightheartedness. You can choose to make your job a game. You can play with your responsibilities and how you go about making decisions. You can hear the little child's voice in your head that endlessly asks, "When are we going to have some fun?" And you can answer, "Right now, my friend!"

CHAPTER 21

"SAY HEY" WILLIE MAYS

"They invented the All-Star Game for Willie Mays."
—Ted Williams, Baseball Legend (1918-2002)

Sometimes, when folks learn of my former work at *The Tonight Show*, they want to know who, of all the famous people I've met, excited me the most. The answer is always Hall of Fame baseball star Willie Mays.

As I mentioned in an earlier chapter I grew up in New York City a big baseball fan. My favorite team from the time I was 10 years old was the New York Giants. Maybe I rooted for them because they were always the "underdog" when I was a kid—and I've always identified with those who have had to struggle to succeed. This was during the early 1950s when the Yankees were the best team in the American League and the Brooklyn Dodgers, the usual frontrunners in the National League. I hated the Dodgers, but I hated the Yankees more, so I decided to root for the only home team that was left, the New York Giants.

My love for the Giants grew in 1951 when they brought rookie Willie Mays—later to be known as the "Say Hey" kid—up to the major leagues. He was an instant "phenom." He also became my baseball hero! As an 11 years old I was still developing my fielding skills. Once I saw Mays' flashy "basket catch" I decided I had to learn to catch a ball that way. The more homeruns he hit, the more bases he stole, the more spectacular fielding plays he made, the more he locked in as my idol. I followed his career into my college years and beyond.

A few years after he retired, NBC decided to do a television Special about his career, and asked *The Tonight Show* to book him as a guest to promote the event. Since I handled most of the sports figures booked on the show, it was a foregone conclusion that I would be assigned the responsibility of producing the Willie Mays segment. There was absolutely no way that anyone else was going to have what I considered this ultimate honor!

It was difficult tracking him down to discuss the interview. NBC had sent him out on a national promotion tour. I spoke to his wife in San Francisco a few times on the phone, asking her to have him call me from the road. As I waited for the call that never came, I realized I didn't really need to speak to him beforehand after all. I knew more about his career than almost anybody else and could compose a good interview.

The day for Willie Mays' appearance finally arrived. I was very excited! The NBC publicity folks told me they had arranged for him to be picked up at the airport by a limousine and transported to our Burbank studios. He would arrive sometime during the afternoon, long before the 5:30 taping.

"Great," I thought. "He'll be here in plenty of time for me to have a nice quality visit with him before the taping begins." I informed the studio security guard to alert me once Willie showed up since our offices were on another part of the NBC lot.

At some point during the afternoon, the security guard phoned to say that Mays had arrived at his dressing room, and I began to make my way down to the studio area. I was nervous. I was about to meet my childhood idol—the man who had given me so many great moments as I was growing up. I was now at the door of his dressing room. I knocked. From inside I heard that "squeaky" voice, familiar to me from all those broadcast interviews I had listened to.

"Who's there?"

"Howard Papush," I replied. "I'm your talent coordinator for tonight's show."

"Oh yes, Howard, come on in."

Perhaps he recognized my name because his wife had told him I had been calling. Or maybe it was just the fact that Howard is his middle name and easy for him to remember. I opened the door and there, standing before me, was my idol Willie Mays. I extended my arm, we shook hands, and I immediately launched into an explanation of that night's show, the order of guests, and a rundown on the questions I had prepared for Johnny to ask him.

But, as before during major moments in my life, I began to hear an insistent voice from deep inside me, whispering in my ear. "This is your idol Willie Mays. You never thought you were ever going to get the chance to meet him and now here he is. And you're playing it like Mr. Cool. You haven't really connected yet. Do something about it!"

Little Howie was indeed talking to me, and he was *so right*! Here was my idol. Here was my chance to let Willie Mays know how important he had been to me as I was growing up. Instantly I stopped briefing him and said simply, "It is such an honor and pleasure to finally meet you. You are my all-time baseball hero. May I shake your hand again?"

My arm was already extended. He looked puzzled but reached out to shake hands again. As our palms touched *this time* I made the psychic connection. Little Howie Papush from Flushing, New York was actually shaking the hand of his idol Willie Mays. What an incredible moment for me! And I had chosen to listen to that kid's voice within me, the voice that knew the significance of this meeting.

What happened that day is similar to situations that happen to all of us frequently. There is a voice that will not be silent. It says important things. We need to listen a little more, because it helps us to be more in balance in our lives.

As I conduct my playshops, and we actually get to romp and cavort, I'm giving everyone in the room the chance to viscerally connect with that little kid inside. The adult part of us is treating the kid part of us to recess, almost like taking him or her to a nearby park for some fun and play. That is why people feel so happy after one of my programs, and very good about themselves. For they have connected with a very important and joyous part of who they are!

CHAPTER 22

ZERO MOSTEL "FIDDLES" AROUND

"I've had a perfectly wonderful evening. But this wasn't it."
—*Groucho Marx, Comedian (1890-1977)*

One of the most frightening and yet more playful moments I experienced during my tenure at *The Tonight Show* occurred the night I shepherded the legendary Zero Mostel through one of his visits to the show.

Zero was world-famous for his rollicking comedy role in the Mel Brooks film, *The Producers*, and his three Tony Award®-winning performances on Broadway in *Rhinoceros, A Funny Thing Happened on the Way to the Forum*, and as Tevya in the classic *Fiddler on the Roof*. He also had a reputation in entertainment circles as being unpredictable, zany and a bit of a clown in his personal life.

When he was booked to appear I volunteered to do the interview, feeling this was one "character" I would like to get to know. So I was a bit surprised when none of those idiosyncrasies showed up in our phone talk or in our face-to-face meeting the night of his appearance. As I went over the notes with him in his dressing room, he was jovial and friendly, and seemed utterly sane. When it came time for his participation on the show we calmly walked backstage and I stood with him exchanging small talk as we waited for the commercial break to end and for Johnny to introduce him. As the band music began to fade (the clue that we were coming out of the commercial) I wished him well, shook his hand, and began to walk away. Suddenly, with a wave of his arm, he started gesturing for me to return.

"Perhaps he's forgotten something," I thought, and hurriedly went to his side. From behind the curtain I could hear Johnny introducing this Broadway legend. Zero was now whispering something into my ear but I couldn't make out what he was saying. It sounded like gibberish. He moved even closer to my face and suddenly grabbed my arm. Johnny was at the end of the intro, the audience was applauding, and our stagehand was about to pull the curtain back to reveal Zero. And Zero had my arm firmly in his grasp. It was obvious now what he was trying to do. His plan was to drag me onstage with him!

I freaked out! It was almost as if my life was passing in front of me. I was sure if I "tumbled" onstage with Zero I would be blamed somehow for having instigated this surprise Papush appearance on the show. With a final great jerk of my arm I was able to pull free and flee. But that night every *Tonight Show* viewer saw a giggling Zero looking towards the wings as my leg disappeared from view.

Returning to my position onstage but off-camera, I could feel my heart thumping in my chest. "What a stunt," I thought to myself, as a wildly manic Zero clowned with Johnny, delivering inane responses to the proper questions I had prepared. The audience seemed to enjoy him very much but I wasn't sure Johnny appreciated his antics, and the talk the next day at the production meeting was about Zero's weird performance. All I could think about was the scary stunt he had tried to pull off the night before.

Zero came back to visit a few months later, and I bravely offered to be his interviewer once again. This gave me the chance to remind and playfully "chastise" him for his former appearance prank. This time, I escorted him backstage, dropped him off, and hurried away so that he couldn't try any new "funny business" with me.

The next year the world was shocked when he died suddenly of a heart attack at the age of 62 and I was very saddened by his passing. But I will always cherish the memory of having worked (and played) with him and to recall that night when he tried to make me part of his act.

I often try to include some zany moments in my seminars. It always adds a note of surprise and delight for the participants. Zero obviously taught me that it was okay for a grown man or woman to be "silly" from time to time and I like to impart that message. In fact I always thank the people who have been the silliest during the seminars, and perhaps for the first time in their lives, they feel honored and acknowledged for being different. The point I am trying to make here is that the act of revealing all facets of your unique personality to your workmates, your neighbors, and your friends is a really good thing.

Have you taken the time to be silly today? Need some more proof? Read on.

CHAPTER 23

THE EVER PLAYFUL MEL BROOKS

> "…if you're alive you've got to flap your arms and legs, you've got to jump around a lot, for life is the very opposite of death. Therefore you must at very least think noisy and colorfully, or you're not alive."
> —Mel Brooks, Actor, Writer, Producer (1926-present)

He is funny, he is playful, he too can be very silly, and he is a wonderful example of an "ageless" child in a grown man's body. He is the one and only Mel Brooks and I will always remember him as the guy who, on one unforgettable day, made me laugh so hard that I almost "peed in my pants."

I had volunteered to be his talent coordinator when he agreed to a booking on *The Tonight Show* in 1974. Mel had been one of Johnny's guests on his very first show on October 1, 1962, but had not returned often since then. Now he was anxious to promote his latest film, *Young Frankenstein*.

When I made my first contact with him he insisted he was too busy writing a new script to be interviewed on the phone. He asked that I come over to the 20th Century Fox lot, where he had an office, and we could talk while he did his other work. Little did I know that I was going to be treated to a wild afternoon of fun.

The Mel Brooks I met that day was gracious and friendly and incredibly funny. He loved telling stories about his life and career, and he had a great memory for names and situations. When he realized I was a fan of his and a good listener, he regaled me with tale after funny tale. Unlike many other guests I had pre-interviewed for the show, he required no prompting. As I took feverish notes he reminisced about his writing days on the classic television series, *Your Show of Shows*. One of the more incredible stories involved the time he so alienated the show's star, Sid Caesar, that Sid literally picked him up and dangled him out the upper story window of a New York City skyscraper, threatening to drop him.

Suddenly changing directions, Mel asked me if I knew why an elderly Jewish man should never try to sing the song, *Dancing in the Dark*. Before I could fathom a guess, he proceeded to explain. "An old Jewish guy will start the song at too high a pitch and then he has nowhere to go. Listen."

And affecting the accented voice of an Eastern European man, Mel began to sing: "Dancing in the dark...." With each line the pitch of his voice rose, struggling to hit the higher notes. Soon he was screeching in a falsetto voice, attempting to get through the song. On paper it's hard to capture how funny this all sounds, but it was hilarious.

Mel Brooks now had me in his power—I was hysterical—and so he started the song again to demonstrate anew why old Jewish men should not sing that song. I was pleading for him to stop, laughing so hard that I knew I was going to lose control of my bladder at any moment. He finally took mercy on me and stopped singing. Hours later I left his office exhausted but armed with notes for five shows. Mel was terrific the night of his appearance. *Dancing in the Dark* had Johnny laughing too until there were tears in his eyes.

My association with Mel Brooks was not limited to his visits to *The Tonight Show*. We used to bump into each other in the oddest of places. One morning we ran past each other along the grassy median on San Vicente Boulevard in Santa Monica as I trained for a 10K race. After that, whenever we talked on the phone, he would first ask me running questions (he was the novice) before we got into the show biz stuff. Unlike many celebrities who may not remember you from one moment to the next, or out of context, he knew exactly who I was whenever we bumped into each other. He started referring to me as HowardPapush (as if my name was one word) whenever we crossed paths, and that seemed to happen often.

About a year after I left *The Tonight Show* I realized that I had always wanted to be a performer, and began to take professional acting classes. I called Mel up one day and asked if I could come over to his office and talk about this career shift. "Sure," he said, "and then we'll go to lunch at the commissary." True to his word we had a nice conversation which continued over lunch. Hanging with Mel on the 20th Century Fox lot that day was quite an experience. Besides the sage acting advice he gave me, Mel created a surreal scene as we were coming out of the commissary.

Former President Gerald Ford, who now sat on the Board of Directors at the studio, suddenly appeared down the path from us. Surrounded by secret servicemen, he was heading towards the private corporate dining room. Mel spotted the ex-President, left my side, and began to make a mad dash towards Ford. The secret servicemen, not recognizing who this man was, scrambled to intercept him, but Brooks was already in front of the former President and, extending his arm for a handshake, exclaimed loud and playfully, "President Ford, *say hello* to Mel Brooks!"

The former President laughed and greeted him warmly, the secret servicemen relaxed the grips on their concealed weapons, and I breathed a sigh of relief. Mel had acted quite spontaneously, just like a kid might do when seeing someone famous, but it could have had serious implications for him.

I appreciate two other things Mel did during that time. First, he set up an audition for me for one of his films and, although I didn't get the part I read for, I was gratified that he was so supportive. The second occurred one morning at a delicatessen in Los Angeles. My older brother was concluding a few days' visit with me from New York and I had taken him out to breakfast before driving him to the airport.

We were enjoying our food when Mel suddenly "breezed" into the place, passed our booth without looking, and stopped a few booths down to greet some acquaintances. As he was finishing his chat with them I said in a loud voice directed at him, "Hey, don't you say hello?" He turned around, saw who it was, and walked right over to our table. Ignoring me and looking my brother right in the eye, he said, "Hi I'm Mel Brooks, and who are you?"

"I'm his brother Joel."

"Howard Papush's younger brother or is it the older brother?" Mel quizzed playfully.

"We're not sure," responded my brother glibly.

"You have some brother there Joel Papush. Do you know he has decided to become an actor and to follow his dream? I think he has a lot of courage and I hope you're proud of him."

Here was this famous, successful multi-talented writer, director, actor giving me such support, and letting my brother know just what he thought of me. I felt so good about myself at that moment and have remembered his kind words to this day.

Mel Brooks is now 78 years old. He has gray, receding hair and his share of wrinkles. So what? Now the toast of Broadway with his record multi-Tony Award®-winning musical comedy, *The Producers*, and currently preparing a musical version of *Young Frankenstein*, he continues to embody the energy, creativity, and zest for life that most kids manifest on a daily basis.

That's the Mel Brooks I first came in contact with in 1974 and nothing has changed. I think of him often when I am preparing my seminars and always try to be as playful as I've always seen him be. No question that Mel Brooks is my role model and indeed the most playful man I ever met.

PART FOUR

FEELING YOUNG— SCALPEL NOT REQUIRED!

CHAPTER 24

THE SEARCH FOR PERPETUAL YOUTH

> "If wrinkles must be written upon your brows, let them not be written upon the heart. The spirit should not grow old."
> —James Garfield, 20th United States President (1831-1881)

Few of us want to grow old. We watched as our parents and relatives turned gray and wrinkled, and listened to them complain about their aches and pains. In our hearts we know that we are aging too and we don't like it. We look in the mirror and can't believe who we see. Inside we may feel like a teenager, or in our early 20s, but the lines on our faces and the emerging bags under our eyes say something different.

Aging is a natural process. It happens to all of us. It was programmed into our genes even as we were developing inside our mothers' wombs. But today's scientists are telling us we do have some choices in the matter. Plastic surgeons and anti-aging professionals purport to have the answers, and people are responding.

In 2001, 8.5 million cosmetic procedures were done in the United States alone. From facelifts to eyelid surgery to tummy tucks to collagen to Botox injections to face peelings—countless individuals are turning to plastic surgeons and other health professionals to re-sculpt their faces and bodies, or find other ways to make them feel better as they grow older.

The media have hopped onto the youth search big-time. A

feature article in *Parade* magazine a few years ago posed the question, "Can We Grow Young?" The data revealed:
- Between 1980 and 1990 the number of people living to be over 100 doubled.
- The average life span has risen from 47 years to 77 since 1900.
- The fastest growing segment of the population is the over-85 category.
- If medical advances continue over the next 30 years, the more than 76 million-plus baby boomers might look forward to celebrating their 100th birthday in good health.
- Life spans of 120 to 130 years may not be unusual.

The article further discussed the work of a group of doctors active with the American Academy of Anti-Aging Medicine who share one fundamental belief—age is inevitable but aging is not.

Dr. Ronald Klatz, president of this group, estimated at the time that Americans spend more than $1 billion on nutritional and drug anti-aging treatments. Klatz said that "the strongest science is behind the antioxidants, especially vitamins A, C, E, and selenium." Anti-oxidants prevent the destruction caused by substances called "free radicals" which can damage cells and lead to cancer, heart disease, and other age-related ailments.

Advocates said that DHEA supplements can boost libido and help prevent heart disease, cancer and memory loss. DHEA, produced by the adrenal gland, is converted into testosterone and estrogen. Levels begin to fall off after age 35. But some studies have shown that a low blood level of DHEA is associated with an increased risk of cardiovascular disease in men older than 50 and an increased risk of breast cancer in women before menopause. A *Journal of the American Medical Association* article concluded that the scientific verdict on DHEA is still not in. Some experts think it is dangerous.

Supplemental testosterone is said to boost energy and libido, build muscle and work other small miracles. By prescription there is human growth hormone (HGH) which supposedly regulates bone and muscle development in children, but can also improve heart and kidney function, boost immunity and preserve lean body mass, advocates say. Klatz thinks human growth hormones may someday make it impossible to differentiate a healthy 65-year old man from a healthy 105-year old.

Also there are other anti-aging remedies and methods with little or no science behind them that have a devoted following:
- "Deer antler velvet" is supposed to have an anabolic effect to improve metabolism. An herbal supplement, and an extract of it called pantocrinum, is used for fatigue.
- A mixture of ginseng and cordyceps is an old-fashioned longevity formula.
- The "chin gym," is a patented mini weightlifting system.
- The "wrinkle patch" infused with vitamin C and applied directly over unwanted lines.
- The "Bio-Flex Magnetic Wrinkle-Reducing Mask" which is supposed to increase circulation to the skin and underlying muscles of the face.

Unfortunately, under the Dietary Supplement Health, and Safety Education Act of 1994, the FDA allows the marketing of supplements—vitamins, herbs, minerals—with certain health claims without the need to submit data.

So what is *your* choice? Will you select the scalpel, the vitamin supplements—perhaps the "chin gym?" Or are you going to opt for the technique that I believe holds the most promise for helping us retain the feeling of youth into our golden years?

What it requires is for you to make sure you're in touch with that most important part of your psyche—the kid inside. You see it is the inner child that is the source of our energies and our passions and our zest for life. It is the part of us that will keep us feeling and thinking young even if the mirror tries to say that we're growing older. And it has a voice that talks to you all the time. Are you listening?

CHAPTER 25

IT'S TIME YOUR INNER CHILD AND I HAD A TALK

"Your inner child needs you to give him your time and attention. By doing this, you will let him know that he has a real champion."
—*John Bradshaw, Best-selling Author (1933-present)*

Often people ask me if I ever get "performance fear" when I'm about to make a presentation. My response is that I probably would if, when I looked out at the sea of faces, I saw only adults looking back at me. But the truth is I actually envision the faces of children out there, peering over the shoulders of what seem the bodies of grownup men and women. And those kids have smiling faces and are eager to hear what I have to say. So why would I be afraid?

As I wrote previously, there are usually three types of people in my audience—the "competitors," the "cautious ones," and a few "cynics." Interestingly you see these three character types on the playground as well. There are the kids who are ready to jump into everything, the kids who hold back until they feel safe, and the few others who keep themselves separated from the group because of their insecurities. Remember the story I told you about "Iguana" with the postal service?

I imagine you fall into groups one and two. But if you do identify with the cynics, I want to thank you for being open to my book as well. Your inner child may be scared but you're still willing to listen and I applaud you for that.

So let's begin the next part of this journey together. I want to have a conversation with your Inner Child. Still not sure he or she exists? Let me verbalize what this child is likely to say on any given Monday morning.

> "I don't want to go to work today. Why don't we go to the beach instead!"

Or else that little voice might show up in the restaurant at lunchtime and ask, "Why are we ordering a salad? Didn't you see the dessert cart over there? Let's have some gooey chocolate cake right now."

When I speak these scenarios in my seminars people instantly start laughing. Come on—who hasn't heard that voice at one time or another? Well, that's your Inner Child talking to you. Kids like to have fun. They don't want to do chores—they want to go to the beach or outside to play. And most kids would certainly pick chocolate cake over something green any day.

Now I'm not suggesting you give in to that voice, cut work and go to the beach (although some days that might be the antidote for having worked much too hard the week before). And I don't believe that a fabulous-looking dessert is as good for you at lunch time as a salad might be. But you don't always have to follow the nutritionist's guidelines perfectly. That's just a couple of examples of your inner kid talking to you. I'm sure you could come up with countless more.

Okay now allow the "inner child" part of you to listen to what I am about to say. I am going to address your *child* directly:

> "Little kid, you are a very important voice that contributes to the total person of everything you really are. You provide the energy, the joy, and the creativity. You're the part that likes to laugh, and the part that likes to connect with others. But so much of the time that other voice, your 'so-called adult' part, doesn't want to listen. That adult may fear that you will get them into trouble, or that you will

> say something that someone else might
> think is inappropriate."

For years my grownup Howard-part kept "Howie" locked in a closet, not wanting to let him come out. I thought I was doing what was best, but I was actually hurting our full potential. Thankfully I sought professional help and experienced how important "Howie" was, and still is, to our total growth. The counseling helped me to see that we are truly a partnership, and that I, as the adult Howard, always need to be there to listen to what's going on with little "Howie." It's the same thing that most parents do to protect their own children when they need assistance. But sometimes it's hard for those grownups to assist themselves.

Let me give you an example from my own life of how this partnership can work very effectively. When I began to market my seminars I noticed that I always got scared whenever I had to go to a first meeting with a potential client. The overriding feeling was that I was going to be late for the appointment. This confused me because I am very time-conscious and always manage to be where I need to be at the appointed hour. But there was a gnawing feeling inside that I was, somehow, going to be late. Of course I never was. Finally one day as I was once again experiencing those anxious moments, I decided to ask little Howie directly if he knew what was going on. Howie, please tell them what you said to me.

> **"Well I told you I was sure we were going to
> be late and I was afraid that the person we
> had the appointment with was going to
> holler at us!"**

At first I was mystified that Howie thought that! I tried to explain that no one would holler at us even if we *were* late—that wouldn't be professional. However, he kept sticking with his fear. So I thought about it, and I thought about it some more, and finally I realized what was really going on.

When I was a kid I used to witness a recurring scene between my parents. They would be preparing to go out for the afternoon or evening and my father would be ready and waiting while my mother meticulously applied her makeup. My father, a "time nut," would become agitated, fearing that they were going to be late for the event. Eventually he would begin to holler at her. I remember how loud his voice was and how upsetting it was for me.

Finally it clicked in my mind what the connection was for little Howie. He saw a business authority figure as being our father. He feared that if we were late (like my mother always was), a director of training or human resources (our father) would holler at us just like my real father had raged at my mom. Once I understood what was really going on I was in a position to dialogue with Howie and explain to him that, although I was sure we would not get hollered at, I was there to protect Howie from the terrible discomfort he had felt as a small boy. I went even further.

Respecting Howie's feelings, I promised him that if we were hollered at I, as the adult Howard, would tell the person doing the hollering to stop it. And if they wouldn't—then we would just get up and leave and not deal with that person again.

> **"That made me feel safe. From then on I stopped getting worried when we had an appointment. I felt that big Howard would take care of me."**

> "Well you didn't stop worrying at first. But the more I expressed it to you the more you believed and trusted me."

This is an example of the dialoguing I do with little Howie, and that you can do as well with your Inner Child. I know it may sound a bit schizophrenic but it's really not. To learn more about your inner child I once again direct you to John Bradshaw's best-seller, *Homecoming: Reclaiming and Championing Your Inner Child*. It was of tremendous help to me in my journey to better self-understanding.

So as we continue this wondrous journey called life it is crucial that we allow that inner child in us—with all that child's spirit, energy and creativity—to play an important role in keeping us young. Otherwise, all the plastic surgery, vitamin pills, and Botox treatments won't matter at all.

CHAPTER 26

REMEMBER WHEN?

"How dear to this heart are the scenes of my childhood, when fond recollection presents them to view."
—*Samuel Woodworth, English Poet (1784-1842)*

When we were kids there were lots of things around that were integral parts of our life. They used to delight, amaze and entertain us. We probably don't think about them much anymore but they were important then. Every generation has its stuff. For those of you in your 40s, 50s and 60s here are a few things that may stir your memories and key you back to your youth.

Remember:
- Catching "fire flies" in a jar
- Indian grips
- Flypaper
- Candy buttons on strips of white paper
- Stoop Ball
- Mucilage
- Dixie Cups with pictures of ball players and movie stars on the lids
- Galoshes
- Roller Skate Keys
- Party Telephone Lines
- Going to the movies and being seated by ladies with flashlights
- Charlotte Russes
- Wax Lips
- Pant Leg Clips so your cuffs didn't get caught in the bicycle chain

- Ice Cream Parlors with plush booths
- Belly-Whopping on your sled
- Rootie Kazootie on TV
- Marbles like "aggies" and "peewees" that you carried in your pocket
- Roasting Potatoes in a pit in the ground
- Nancy Drew and the Hardy Boys
- Candy wax bottles with sweet "goo" inside that you drank
- Antonino "Argentine" Rocca wrestling in his bare feet
- "Smoking" punks
- Dick and Jane and Spot and Puff
- "Olly olly oxen free"
- '57 Chevys
- Going Steady
- Ovaltine
- The Peanut Gallery
- "I Want My Maypo"
- Chinese Hand Ball
- Spin The Bottle
- Building Forts
- "Johnny On The Pony"

When you think of these things it is actually the little kid inside of you who is doing the reminiscing. He or she is still riveted back to the time when you were a child. It is "your kid" who is smiling, saying, "Yes, whatever happened to those candy wax bottles?" or "Wouldn't it be great to go belly-whopping just one more time?"

Let's have some more fun, and a little challenge. I'm going to give you a "pop quiz" (remember them?) to see just how much you know about some of our favorite toys and games from yesteryear. Actually you're probably going to learn lots of things about these playthings we took for granted while we were growing up. Here goes:

1. Q. When was the first electric toy train invented?
    A)   1900
    B)   1885

C) 1915
2. Q. Who created that train set?
   A) Joshua Lionel Cowen
   B) Samuel Pullman
   C) Henry Locomotiff
   D) None of the above
3. Q. How many Crayola crayons come off the assembly line each year?
   A) 7 Million
   B) 500 Million
   C) 2 Billion
4. Q. "Hello, boys! Make lots of toys." That was the headline in the national ads for what new toy in 1913?
   A) Tinker Toys
   B) Erector Sets
   C) Lincoln Logs
5. Q. What son of the following famous man developed the first set of Lincoln Logs?
   A) Ulysses S. Grant
   B) John Astor
   C) Frank Lloyd Wright
6. Q. Why did a man named Charles Darrow invent the game of "Monopoly?"
   A) As the owner of several hotels in Atlantic City he wanted to promote the idea of vacationing there.
   B) He was Clarence Darrow's son and he wanted to make a name for himself in another profession.
   C) As an out-of-work guy he was longing to recall the fun he once had as a child.
   D) None of the above.
7. Q. What toy was created by a marine engineer who, while working on a testing meter to measure horsepower on battleships, had a piece of material he was using fall off and bounce across the floor?
8. Q. When did the Pez candy dispensers first appear on the market?
   A) 1940s
   B) 1950s

C) 1960s
9. Q. When were shoe roller skates first invented?
    A) 1860s
    B) 1890s
    C) Early 1900s
10. Q. How did historians come to learn about the Yo-Yo?
    A) They traced it to ancient China.
    B) They discovered it on a drawing on a Grecian vase in 500 B.C.
    C) They learned that it had been used as a weapon in the Philippines for 400 years.
    D) All of the above
11. Q. When was the first jigsaw puzzle created?
    A) Before World War I
    B) Before the Revolutionary War
    C) Before the Civil War
12. Q. Who is older—Mr. Potato Head or Barbie?

THE ANSWERS:
1. A) The electric toy train first came out in 1900. It consisted of one wooden car that ran around a circular track. The first accessory, a suspension bridge, was issued two years later, followed the next year by the Baltimore & Ohio locomotive. Nearly 1 million engines, cabooses and other rolling stock are produced annually. That's enough to make a toy train nearly 50 miles long.
2. A) Joshua Lionel Cowen invented the first toy electric train.
3. C) More than 2 billion Crayolas are made each year. They were first manufactured in 1903. The average American child wears down 730 crayons by the age of 10. Crayola was derived from French and means "oily chalk." When first manufactured the box contained 8 colors; 64 were introduced in 1958.
4. B) Erector sets used the slogan, "Hello, boys! Make lots of toys." Though little boys were the early targets, things have changed. For instance, the winners of a national contest in 1993 were five little girls from Brooklyn, New York who built a bridge.
5. C) John Lloyd Wright, son of architect Frank Lloyd Wright,

conceived the idea of Lincoln Logs after viewing the Imperial Hotel in Tokyo.

6. C) It was during the Depression that the unemployed Darrow created "Monopoly" as he was reminiscing about his childhood days in Atlantic City. The game is now licensed in 33 countries and printed in 23 different languages.

7. The falling material morphed into the "Slinky." The engineer watched in amazement as the spring tumbled end-over-end. He took the spring home and worked out a steel formula that allowed the spring to "walk." More than 250 million of them have been sold since 1945.

8. B) Pez machines first showed up in the 1950s. Today some of them are so popular that several price guides have been published. A rare bride-and-groom set can cost over $600.

9. A) Shoe skates were first seen in January of 1866. Everett Barney took out the first patent for clamp skates. They were 4-wheeled metal things that hooked around the soles of your shoes. (Sorry, but I can't tell you anything about that indispensable skate key that we hung around our necks.)

10. D). This type of toy can be traced back to *all* those cultures. Also, the term, Yo-yo, means "come, come" or "come back" in Tagalog, one of the Filipino language dialects. A wooden yo-yo was first made in California by a Filipino, Pedro Flores in the 1920s. Plastic models were introduced in 1957.

11. B) The jigsaw puzzle first appeared before the Revolutionary War. John Spilsbury, a London engraver and mapmaker, produced the first puzzle around 1760. He mounted one of his maps on a sheet of hardwood and cut around the borders using a fine-bladed saw.

12. Mr. Potato Head is older. He's 53. Barbie is only 45.

CHAPTER 27

AND NOW A WORD FROM THE SPONSORS

"Make it simple. Make it memorable. Make it inviting to look at. Make it fun to read."
—Leo Burnett, U.S. Advertising Executive (1891-1971)

I'm constantly amazed at how often the advertising community creates ads and commercials to sell their clients products or services by appealing to that child within all of us. I'm sure you've seen some of them.

Do you remember 2002 Nike's "Tag" television commercial? It was named the world's best from over 5000 entries from 61 countries at the 49th International Advertising Festival. Adults are shown playing "Tag," chasing each other around the subways, office buildings, and streets of a major city. The spot ends with the simple one word message, "Play."

It narrowly beat out a commercial from Xbox Europe with a similar theme. That one depicted a newborn baby shot out of a window, aging rapidly and landing in a grave. The tag line—"Life is short, play more."

Hotel chains have gotten into the action big time. Embassy Suites for a long time ran an ad in *USA TODAY* that caught readers' attention with this headline, "This weekend, be a kid again." Pictured in the ad was a "Weekend To-Do List":

1. Stay up late
2. Jump on bed
3. Play tent
4. Watch scary movies
5. Run rampant through two-room suite

6. Sleep in
7. Eat a lot of free breakfast
8. Dive-bomb Rubber Ducky in bathtub
9. Leave wet towels on floor
10. Repeat steps 1-9

Then Renaissance Hotels launched their "Whatever happened to recess?" campaign. They talked about their "Come Out and Play" Weekend rates and stated that it was the "perfect time to put the 'homework' aside."

Travelodge, in their ads, once took an approach that never mentioned "play" or "recess" but nevertheless was appealing to our fun side, with some surprising scientific facts to impart. The headline: "It takes 43 muscles to frown vs. 17 to smile. Here's a few new ways we plan to give your face a rest."

The ad then lists all the things they're going to provide that will "bring a refreshing smile to your face." Among their perks—fresh coffee in the room, a complimentary newspaper, no charge for local phone calls and no access charges for long-distance calls.

The Rancho Bernardo Inn, a resort in San Diego, promoted their establishment with the headline, "A resort that believes in letting kids be kids, and letting adults be even bigger kids." The copy: "If you ask us, fun and relaxation should be activities open to all age groups" and extolled the championship golf course, the unlimited greens fees, the tennis, the spa, and the included meals that go with the patron's stay.

How about the automobile ads? Recall the 1998 one from Toyota? "The call of the wild whispers your name, and asks if you can come out and play." Smack dab in the middle of the page is a photo of the 4 Runner, Toyota's Suburban Utility Vehicle.

That campaign must have worked. The next year they were at it again with this headline: "The auto show. Proof you don't have to be a child to play with big trucks and cool cars." And the copy that followed: "With the new full-size Tundra and new Camry Solara to enjoy, Toyota's auto show display is like your fountain of youth. That's where you'll find this truck and coupe, as well as our vast collection of 1999 models. C'mon, why should kids have all the fun?"

Not to be outdone, auto maker Saab declared in one of their ads, "Studies indicate parents need toys, too." The copy: "Yes, you need plenty of room for the kids. And more room for their stuff. And, of course, you need the peace of mind that comes from a company with a long history of setting automotive safety standards. But any psychologist worth his beard will tell you that's not enough. To be your normal, happy, well-balanced self, you also need something more. Something thrilling. Fun. Something that sticks to the road like bubble gum to hair. A big, beautiful honking toy that you and your family will enjoy, otherwise known as the Saab 900 S 5-door."

Tell me that ad was not speaking to someone's Inner Child. The next year they had a new headline, "Saab vs. Recess," with the follow-up banner, "The car that can make driving feel like playing."

Automobiles needn't be regulation size either! Here is a former ad from The Sharper Image gift stores. The headline: "Parking lot full? Try your desk." Then, over a photo of a cherry red Porsche, the copy says: "That empty space beside your pencil sharpener would be ideal for this sleek 1:18-scale Boxster. Select from over 30 collectible die-cast models at The Sharper Image—and invest in some powerful daydreams. Because now you can own every car you ever wanted. At least until your desk fills up."

What about the advertisers who wanted you to buy Timex watches? They were very subtle with their sales pitch. There was just a photo of two cross-country skiers on their way into a snow covered meadow. The caption above: "You're not in third grade anymore. Take as many recesses as you want."

Or let's appeal to your sense of wanderlust. Superimposed over a photo of a cute lamb, the Welsh travel board presented this headline: "Wales brings out the child in anyone—nights in private castles, mornings at the seashore, afternoon frolics with lambs and ponies in the endless green."

My favorite ad of all was a campaign for the Home Depot to lure customers into their stores. Above a full page of photos of lawn mowers, hedge trimmers, leaf blowers, and chain saws was the giant headline, "MAKES YOU WANNA GO OUTSIDE AND

PLAY." A sub-headline half-way down the page continued the theme, "Turn your yard into a playground."

That sure motivated me. Anyone wanting to purchase several unused hedge trimmers, or a really neat Electric Rear Bag Mulching Mower, please let me know as soon as you can at drplay@doctorplay.com. Yep, they're in their original boxes...

CHAPTER 28

HOW DO YOU SPELL "NEOTENOUS"?

"The idea is to die young as late as possible."
—Ashley Montagu, Anthropologist (1905-1999)

As I have mentioned previously, during my time at *The Tonight Show* many famous and accomplished people swirled around me. I met screen idols, brilliant scientists, the successful pop singers of the day, noted authors, funny comedians, opera stars, and sports legends.

Of particular fascination was anthropologist and author Ashley Montagu, who, ironically, I never officially met, because he worked with a different talent coordinator. At the time he was in his early 70s, with energy and spark that so lit up the stage, it made him appear much younger. He was one of Johnny's favorite guests: he was bright, amusing, erudite, and always "up." When his name started cropping up as I was researching this book, I finally realized why I had been so drawn to him back then.

What I learned was astounding. Although he had a Ph.D. in anthropology, he had also taught anatomy in American medical schools for over twenty years back in the 40s, and was the man who worked out the embryology of the upper jaw, now used by surgeons to repair cleft palates.

I knew he was a prolific author but wasn't aware that his books touched on such wide-ranging themes as the human significance of love, the fallacy of race, the equality of the sexes, the significance of birth order, the emancipation of the disabled, and the nurturing of children.

It is information in his book, *Growing Young*, that most

stimulates me. He discusses the concept of "neoteny," or the retention of juvenile characteristics in the adult. He believed that these neotenous traits, for example—curiosity, sense of wonder, playfulness, imagination, joyfulness, creativity, open-mindedness, sense of humor, flexibility, resiliency, laughter and tears, optimism, honesty, compassion, sensitivity, trust—are the type of qualities that help people function more effectively as adults. He applauds those of us who have retained our childlike ways for he believes it is a prime mechanism to keep us young. It undoubtedly worked for him as well. Ashley Montagu didn't die until late 1999 when he was 94 years old.

All through this section of my book I am appealing to that inner child of yours to "come out and play," and be a true partner with your adult persona. Now let me take this a step further. Here is a fascinating quiz from *Longevity* magazine's September 1990 edition that was developed with the assistance of Professor Montagu. It will help you to determine just how attuned you are to the child lurking within you, and what you might have to do to bring more of those "neotenous" qualities to the surface.

This is fun, so get a pencil and a piece of paper and let's begin. First write the numbers 1 to 25 down the left side of the page and get ready to score yourself.

HOW NEOTENOUS (CHILDLIKE) ARE YOU?

Read the following declarations and ask yourself how these statements apply to you personally. Use the following set of numbers to score yourself:

4 = I *strongly* agree
3 = I agree
2 = I disagree
1 = I *strongly* disagree

THE STATEMENTS:
1. I am very intuitive and often know what others are thinking or feeling.
2. I cry easily.
3. I laugh easily and often.

4. I have a good sense of humor.
5. I have at least one close friend or family member with whom I share my dreams and fears.
6. People enjoy being with me.
7. I like people, especially those who are different from me.
8. I touch and hug things.
9. I love children.
10. I love animals.
11. I enjoy singing and dancing.
12. I participate in sports or exercise *primarily for fun*.
13. I enjoy solving problems.
14. I'm always thinking of new and better ways to do things.
15. I'm curious about what causes things and makes them work.
16. I enjoy the challenge of new ideas—especially those that challenge my own.
17. I'm interested in many different subjects.
18. I'm stimulated by change and enjoy taking risks.
19. I consider my work interesting, fun or meaningful.
20. I regard my work as play.
21. I have a means of expressing myself creatively.
22. I have an active fantasy life and enjoy daydreaming.
23. I know how to have fun.
24. I expect good things to happen and look forward to the future.
25. I'm generally happy and enjoy life.

Now add all the numbers to come up with your final score. Let's see how you did.

THE RESULTS:
76-100: According to Dr. Montagu, if you have scored over 75, you have managed to retain many life-enhancing and often life-sustaining *neotenous* qualities. You are open, optimistic and warm; gregarious and creative. Sometimes you're even seen as being a bit eccentric. Your enthusiasm is contagious, and others enjoy your presence. These qualities not only boost your immune system and prevent disease, but also aid recovery from injuries and illness. You

probably look younger than most people your age, and certainly think younger.

50-75: Having sacrificed some of your childlike qualities on the road to maturity, you are an *average adult.* It's not so much a matter of knowing how to enjoy life, as it is finding the time, energy or motivation to do so. Responsibilities and life stresses have diminished your capacity for joy, which may seem frivolous next to more serious concerns. You're prone to stress-related symptoms like headaches, backaches, sleep disturbances, and frequent illnesses. But you can increase your pleasure and improve your health by re-discovering and following your natural inclinations toward joy. The key is *immediate gratification.* Don't postpone your happiness by waiting for problems to be solved, savings to accumulate. Today is the perfect day to start living a happy, healthy and long life.

25-49: If you scored below 50, it's time to re-evaluate your life and to re-discover and *nurture* the child within yourself. According to Professor Montagu, in many cases this level of unhappiness is most likely due to *not* getting enough love as a child. Love is the root of all *neotenous* qualities, and the child who has not received adequate love cannot hope to grow into a happy, loving adult. But the good news is you can learn to be a loving person simply by acting like a loving person. When you do, all of the other childlike qualities will be reborn within you.

Don't despair if you didn't score 100. Even Dr. Play has a ways to go before I'm fully able to embrace all those wonderful qualities that my inner child is directing me towards. But remember life is always a journey. I, like you, am doing the best I can.

PART FIVE

GO TO WORK AND PLAY

CHAPTER 29

CREATING FUN IN THE WORKPLACE

"The more joy we have, the more nearly perfect we are."
— *Baruch Spinoza, Dutch Philosopher (1632-1677)*

One of my all-time favorite individuals is Sylvia Woodside, who used to be a human resources manager for the United States Postal Service. She gave me my very first opportunity to show postal workers how to make their work fun. Sylvia once sent me a page from her "More of Life's Little Instructions" daily calendar, noting that I'd probably like the sentiment. The page stated, "Don't expect to play on Saturday if you haven't practiced during the week."

I believe people should go to work with the notion that they're going to be able to have a good time, long before the weekend arrives. There are lots of ways you can make the workplace a fun experience. If you're the owner of a company or the human resources director, or an event planner here are a few suggestions:

THE FUN COMMITTEE
Establish a "fun committee" to keep the company morale high. Use the suggestions I make in the upcoming chapter 34, "20 Fun Games for the Office," to create playshops. Invite groups of 20-30 each month to participate.

HAPPY PLAY DAY
Create a special event for a designated employee (employee of the month, etc.). That person and five of their co-workers get to

go on an all expenses paid mystery trip to an amusement park or other fun destination.

PLAY STATIONS
These are rooms or spaces set up as "romper rooms" for adults. The site can be stocked with jigsaw puzzles, box games, wooden blocks, finger paint sets, and modeling clay. On one wall have a bulletin board of "outrageous employee photographs." Provide throwaway cameras for folks to take candid photos and every few months create a contest to see who has shot the wildest new photo. Yes it's okay to have a coffee station and water cooler there too.

SKIT DAY
Twice a year departments compete for prizes around a central theme related to the company's business.

COSTUME DAY
Held four times a year to coincide with the onset of spring, summer, fall and winter with prizes awarded for the most creative costumes related to a changing theme.

PLAY WITH YOUR FOOD DAY
Have special fun days in the company cafeteria or snack area involving unique menus, ice cream sundaes, a blowing-bubbles-in-your-ice-tea competition, a pie eating contest.

WELLNESS LUNCHES
Employees get a free lunch if they attend a seminar designed to show them how to manage stress by being more playful at work and at home.

MILK AND COOKIES BREAK
Selected groups take a 30-minute break to discuss, with the "fun committee," how to create more joy in the workplace. Hold it once a month and make sure you have a large array of different snacks.

THE FIELD TRIP
Just like when we were kids in school, once or twice a year the company organizes a special field trip for deserving employees. Buses transport the individuals to museums, theme parks, botanical gardens.

CELEBRATIONS JUST BECAUSE…
Periodically have the "fun committee" create an informal celebration to honor some special deed an employee has performed, or a milestone that has been reached. It might be a special wedding anniversary, the birth of a child, a new business contract, the running of a marathon by an employee, some sort of charitable work, whatever.

CHAPTER 30

MY TOY IS BIGGER THAN YOUR TOY

"The supreme accomplishment is to blur the line between work and play."
—Arnold Toynbee, British Economist (1852-1883)

Playing with toys is another wonderful way to get in touch with that kid who lives in your heart. During my "playshops" I always inquire whether the assembled participants have toys sitting on their office desks. More and more folks are saying "yes." That pleases me. At the end of the seminar I make everyone pledge that, within the week, they will secure a new plaything for themselves. One of my favorite things to do is to return to the workplace several days later to view the toys people have bought for themselves. Most people are excited to show off their new acquisitions. Usually the workaholics—who still "haven't gotten around to it"—are embarrassed and plead for more time.

There are studies to back up the notion that toys in the office are of major benefit. Northwestern National Life Insurance Company in Minneapolis directed a two-year national study on employee stress and burnout. It concluded that "toys and playfulness in the workplace reduce stress and enhance creativity." Peggy Lawless, research project director for the study, stated: "If workers are under a great deal of pressure and they know they can take a break and do something completely different to relax, they are more productive."

Experts also say that companies that want to deliver better products and services in a competitive marketplace are finding they have to think differently about problems. Toys, they believe, are great tools in the creative process.

Toys are also great energy boosters and fun things to play with while having serious and perhaps stressful conversations on the phone. Some people say they find it relaxing to do something with their hands while they're solving workplace issues. One day I had an initial meeting with the vice president of human resources for a large restaurant chain. When I walked into his office I spotted a large toy truck sitting on the credenza behind his desk. During our conversation I asked him why the truck was there. His answer: "I have a young son and sometimes he comes to work with me and I needed something here for him to play with."

"And you never play with that truck?" I inquired, although I already sensed the answer. "Well sometimes," was his sheepish and almost apologetic reply. But it shouldn't be that way. People should be proud of their office toys.

The first time I entered the office of City of Beverly Hills' human services director April Meadow for a preliminary meeting I was overwhelmed by her collection of stuffed animals. They were everywhere—it seemed as if I had climbed into an adult play pen. It was great! Instinctively I grabbed a stuffed lion that had caught my eye, propped it on my lap, and told April in no uncertain terms that I was going to play with that toy while I told her about my program. She didn't flinch. In fact I know she loved the idea that I wanted to play with her toys. Within months I was hired to do a series of programs for Beverly Hills personnel that included the city manager, the chief of police, the head of library services, the fire chief, and hundreds of city personnel.

Some time ago, I realized that, while I was lecturing others about the need for toys in their office, I didn't have a special plaything of my own. I vowed to change that, but couldn't seem to find anything that really captured my imagination. Then one day as I looked at some model room settings in an IKEA furniture store (it's a fun thing for me to do), I turned a corner and there in front of me was a display of packaged wooden blocks. Instantly I recalled that, as a kid, I used to love playing with a set of blocks that was part of our toy collection at home. Here was the *perfect* plaything for me.

But something strange began to happen. Two voices were talking in my head simultaneously. One voice (obviously my inner child) was very excited.

"Oh, this is going to be great. I'll have so much fun with these blocks."

But almost instantly another voice interrupted.

"No you won't! You'll play with them for a day or two and then you'll just forget them."

Here was that practical adult voice. The dialogue continued:

"No, that's not true. I'll play with them a lot. I really want them."

"You say that now but it will be just a waste of money because you won't use them."

"They don't cost much at all and I will play with them."

"Let's just forget this nonsense and be on our way."

Now you may think I am being overly dramatic, but I'm not. This is exactly what happened in that aisle at IKEA. From my research I have learned that it's vitally important to use both sides of our brain. Many of us look at the world most with our left, closed-mode model. It's our need to be purposeful and practical. I see it as the voice of the adult.

In contrast our right brain is where so much of our creativity, our joy, and our humor are. It is the voice of the child for me. And it was these two voices which were in conflict. Who was going to win—the practical adult or the pleading kid? I am happy to report that the adult relinquished control and bought the blocks for the excited kid. I am also happy to say that I play with those blocks all the time.

When I'm not out giving seminars I spend a lot of time marketing the program. "No one is going to hire me if they don't know about me," I am always telling myself. So in the early years I used to send my press packet to key contacts at corporations and associations throughout the country. Now I try to obtain their email addresses and alert them to my www.letsplayagain.com website. This gives them a chance to review the material before I call to see if I can set up a phone or in-person appointment. Most of the time I get voice mail. You know, "This is such and such. I'm not here right now but your call is very important to me. Please leave your name and phone number and I'll get back to you as soon as possible."

So I leave a message reminding them who I am, that I sent information to them, and include my phone number. But do they call me back? Not often. So I wait a few days and then make a repeat call. Once again I get their voice message. This is the new office game. It's not "telephone tag"—it's "telephone non-connect." When I was a talent executive at *The Tonight Show* I got lots and lots of calls. And I returned them all. That was the courteous thing to do.

But we're living in a different world. And to me it's very frustrating and very stressful. Now I have my set of wooden blocks to sit and play on the floor with after a series of non-connections. I take my "recess" and have the best time. After 15 minutes or so, I'm ready to make more phone calls, and this time I'm usually feeling creative and playful, and I leave wild and funny messages that often get responses.

I once read something in a magazine that really thrilled me. The world-famous American architect Frank Lloyd Wright credited a toy his mother gave him as a child as a decisive influence on his later career choice. It was a set of wooden blocks! (Now I know why I've always felt so connected to Wright).

The story went on to discuss the work of German educator Friedrich Froebel, the man who invented those objects, as well as many other toys, to stimulate learning. He was also responsible for setting up the first kindergarten. His book, *The Education of Man* (1826), had a profound effect on the approach to early childhood education. He was one of the first to believe in the development of intelligence and character through "play" rather than school.

So here's my assignment, dear reader. Tomorrow, or the next day, or this weekend, I want you to go out and buy a toy. It can be for your office, your car, or your home. Get something that delights you, perhaps a toy that you used to play with when you were young. It will make all the difference in the world. It will de-stress you, it will make you smile and laugh, and it will make your journey home from the office easier.

Here are just a few suggestions:
1. Toys or playthings that will calm you—a "kush" ball or any form of stress ball, a Zen garden, a house plant.
2. Playthings that re-connect you to your childhood—sports objects such as a baseball, basketball, fielder's mitt, tennis racket; a set of jacks, a Barbie doll, jump rope, bag of marbles, crayons, Slinky, finger paints, paste.
3. Objects that make you laugh or smile—toys that play music or give off sound effects; stuffed animals that do outrageous things when you squeeze them.
4. Things that will remind you of how you like to play as an adult—gardening tools, a golf ball or club, knitting yarn, a bottle of olive oil that you use in your gourmet kitchen, whatever.
5. Stuff that makes you feel good—photos of your children or pets, a candy dispenser, a Beanie Baby.

Now aren't you getting excited, contemplating what new item is going to be sharing your workspace or your commute? Wow, I wish I had a cut of the profits stores like Toys R Us, Natural Wonders, and KB Toys have earned from all the business I've sent them. Hey, please write and tell me what you bought.

CHAPTER 31

PLAYING WITH YOUR FOOD

> "You don't get ulcers from what you eat. You get them from what's eating you."
> —*Vicki Baum, Austrian-US Novelist-Screenwriter (1888-1960)*

Lunchtime is a perfect part of the day to catch up on your need to play. Perhaps you had a long, wonderful weekend and work is not doing it for you today. Or you've sat through several excruciating meetings, going over lots of items that were discussed endlessly last week. Still clear in my mind are those long, boring and usually ineffective meetings I was required to attend during my corporate days.

So you're heading out for lunch in retreat, perhaps with a coworker or two, to your favorite Italian restaurant down the block. Make sure you check out the dessert cart before you find your seat. Let your internal kid's voice go wild with all the scrumptious things on display.

Once you've gotten your menu, perused all the offerings, and the waiter arrives at your table, I suggest you begin a playful interaction. Before he or she even has a chance to greet you, declare, "We'll have our check, please." Everyone at your table will laugh, the waiter will smile (hopefully), and the subsequent service will be terrific.

You order the lasagna. "And what will you have to drink?" the waiter asks.

A great fun reply is, "Could I have a hot chocolate?" As he quizzically looks up from his notepad, just smile and ask how his day has been so far. He will probably have a great comeback—

something like, "It's been good *up to now!*" But a connection has just occurred and I bet your lunch will be lots of fun.

Here are some other ways to make the event even more joyful. Now that you have changed your drink order to iced tea, unwrap the straw that arrives alongside it and begin blowing bubbles into your beverage. Yep, you heard me right, begin blowing bubbles! It's that playfully silly thing we used to like to do with our milk at the dining table as we were growing up—the thing designed to make our parents nuts. They usually told you to "stop playing with your food and finish!" But I'm asking you to try and erase that childhood memory still lodged in your brain. Instead, create some fun at the table, lighten your mood, and realize that, because you are now a grownup, you have permission to do whatever you please!

Perhaps the day so far has been worse than just a few boring, frustrating meetings. Maybe you've had a testy conversation on the phone with one of your business clients, or your boss is giving you some major grief. You're sitting at the dining table and you have a major headache. Try this. Order a side of mashed potatoes. When it comes, mash them even more. That's right. Take your fork to them and really mash them. Now I'm not suggesting you fantasize your boss's head under the pressure of your fork, or am I? The point: this is a socially accepted way to relieve some major tension.

Do order that dessert that looked so spectacular on the cart. If you're full you can always order it to go. There will come a time during the afternoon when you may feel hungry again. A bite out of some tiramisu then might serve you well.

Speaking of those long afternoons at work, when a nap or some milk and cookies might be just the best thing, why not institute the "Dr. Play Official Fruit Break" at your place of business. If you're the boss this will be easy to do and it will make the troops like and respect you even more. If you're just a worker bee, take the initiative anyway. It will create lots of good will and be a plus for all concerned.

Bring a piece of ripe fruit from home along with a pretty plate. It can be a banana, an apple, a peach, a pear, a whatever. Just select something large enough that can be cut into several pieces. At three o'clock, start circulating around the floor. Gently saunter into a colleague's office or cubicle. Encourage him to get off the phone, if that's what you find him doing. Offer him a slice of fruit, sit down and chat about something unrelated to business. Maybe you could ask him what his favorite fruit is generally, how his kids did in their soccer game the past weekend, or whether he's played golf (his favorite pastime) recently. Spend a few minutes with him, and then move on to the next office. Eventually all of your office mates are going to look forward to these informal fruit breaks. This is a subtle form of team-building that works well.

Food breaks are important parts of the day. Even if you're a very busy executive you must strive to get up from your desk, get out of your office, and eat something that will nurture (not necessarily nourish) you for the rest of the day. President Ronald Reagan was fond of jelly beans; the first George Bush likes pork rinds; Bill Clinton fancied his cheeseburgers. It's not the food that's important—it's just the act of giving you some time to take a breather. Once done you'll go back to your assignments with renewed vigor. Now go and play with your food!

CHAPTER 32

SKIP, SKIP... SKIP TO THE LOO

"I still get wildly enthusiastic about little things. I play with leaves. I skip down the street and run against the wind."
—Leo Buscaglia, American Writer (1924-1998)

Another way to relieve stress is to do some of the activities you got involved in when you were a kid. There's a cartoon strip that I have that provides a solid reminder. It's a short story line from *Hagar the Horrible*. Throughout the four panels he is moving his body awkwardly, trying to accomplish something that the reader doesn't yet understand. He keeps saying things like: "No, that's not it! Nope. Definitely Not! No Darn! That's not it either!" Finally, in the last panel he exclaims,

> "It's sad—I've tried so hard to be a grownup
> that I've forgotten how to skip!"

Skipping is a lost art for adults. When we were kids we skipped all the time. Watch little kids in the neighborhood or at the mall. At some point you will see them skipping. It comes naturally. We as adults need to skip more. It gets us out of the doldrums. I always tell my seminar attendees that skipping is a great way to de-stress yourself. There is no way you won't begin to smile or laugh while skipping. Try it you'll see.

However, here is a word of caution. Perhaps you might want to begin *surreptitiously,* selecting an area of the workplace where no one else can see you. You know one of those long unfrequented corridors. Or maybe you just want to flaunt the fact that, at your advanced age, you can still skip. The point is you'll feel a lot better once you've done it. It's a form of recess that really works.

There's even a website called www.iskip.com which extols the fun and joy of skipping, the different ways to skip (fast skippers, bouncy skippers, low impact skippers, sassy skippers), the physical and spiritual benefits, and how to react to people who disapprove of what you're doing. They have a report on industrial controls distributor, Charles Emmett McGoff, a 70-year-old skipper from Decatur, Georgia. According to his wife Dorothy, Charles has been skipping as an adult for more than 45 years and picks malls, hospital corridors, and parking lots to perform his fun. Charles' son Pat thinks, "It's a lifelong ploy on his part to be able to claim the insanity defense for a crime he hasn't committed yet." It turns out that his wife was attracted to him initially by his skipping. As she recalls:

> "I remember the first time I saw Charlie—it was at a park in St. Louis called Castlewood. He looked like a 6'4" James Dean, cigarette and all, as he approached the pool. Then he broke out in a skip and it made me laugh at the sight and I just had to meet him. Thus began our courting which ultimately led to our marriage. Eight children and thirteen grandchildren later he still makes my heart skip."

So go ahead, start skipping—even to the bathroom when you have to—and if anyone gives you a hard time, tell them that Dr. Play says it's alright because he *skips* too!

CHAPTER 33

THE "PRAISE" GAME

> "Outstanding leaders go out of their way to boost
> the self-esteem of their personnel. If people believe
> in themselves, it's amazing what they can accomplish."
> —Sam Walton, American Retailing Executive (1918-1992)

We all *have to* work, except for those very, very few who inherit sufficient wealth, and choose to live a life of leisure. Most of us, though, start off having after-school and summer jobs during our teenage years. Then it's on to college or trade school, or we fall into a job that becomes a career. Many of us ultimately find the kind of work that stimulates and pleases. Some of us eventually become parents and choose to stay at home, taking on the challenging career of raising our children to be productive human beings. Sometimes people are faced with having to do both, finding themselves juggling their functions as both parent and employee.

In my role as a motivational speaker I meet many people at corporate events and professional associations who feel that they're not getting enough praise or recognition for the job they do. After a while it makes the whole work experience a difficult one for them. Because of this I'm always exhorting CEO's and company managers to make sure they let their employees know how much they mean to them. These gestures are so important and create such good feelings. Unfortunately fewer and fewer bosses are doing this.

I can remember a specific moment during the time I was working for Ralph Edwards, the creator of such successful television shows as *This Is Your Life* and *Truth or Consequences*, which illustrates this theme. We were involved in an "off the wall" daily television series called, *So You Think You Got Troubles?!*, in its first year of syndication. We were hoping desperately for good ratings and a chance to complete the full season. We had already shot about 70 shows, and we were waiting for a possible pickup so that Ralph and Stu Billett, his producing partner, could savor a successful match to their other hit program, *The People's Court.*

One afternoon in mid-November, Ralph's longtime secretary came into my office clutching a stack of envelopes. She leafed through them until she found the one that was addressed to me. As she smiled and departed, I opened it up and inside was this note:

> Dear Hearts of the 8th and 10th Floor,
> Thanksgiving greetings to each of you.
> Since neither "Court" nor "Troubles"
> has had a real turkey this year, we
> thought we'd send one along. Our love
> and appreciation go with it and the trimmings.
> Much Thanksgiving to you,
> Ralph and Stu

Inside the envelope was a gift certificate for $50 from one of the best supermarket chains in Los Angeles. This wonderful gesture and their recognition of the job we had all done touched me.

But it didn't stop there. A month later I, along with all the staff, was invited by Ralph and his wife to their 42nd annual Christmas-Holiday Office Party in the Cecil B. DeMille Room at the Hollywood Brown Derby restaurant. The invitation asked us to wear our "party clothes." In playful fashion it added: "It's a family party, so we confine it to a spouse (yours), or live-in mate."

At some point during the festivities, Ralph took the microphone and proposed a toast to all his employees, thanking us for all the hard work we had put into the two projects. Now here was a "class act," an employer who truly believed what Sam Walton of the Wal-Mart stores said years ago (review the quote above).

But I had many jobs in the television industry and many bosses who never praised the work of their employees. This used to upset me a lot and I made sure I wasn't that kind of leader when I became a producer.

What do you do though when you're working for an unappreciative boss, and you know you're doing a great job? You certainly can *leave* if you're not getting the kind of "strokes" that you feel you need. Or you can take care of it all by yourself. Once again it involves talking to that "little child" inside. He or she is the part of you who feels neglected or ignored. Tell him what a wonderful job he is doing and how important he is to the workplace.

So many times I found that when I started to recognize and praise myself, magically I got compliments from the boss and others! It really worked. Try it. And also realize that work is a wondrous gift. Let me share an anonymous essay that came into my hands a few years ago. I use it at the end of my seminars on occasion to highlight the work/play balance I feel is so necessary in our lives:

> "In a factory in England all the men pushed their wheelbarrows except one slow worker who pulled his. A surprised visitor asked the foreman why.
>
> "Oh him," the foreman shrugged, "He hates the sight of the bloomin' thing." Unfortunately, a lot of people plod through life hating the sight of their work. It's too bad. Work occupies too much of everyone's time to be hated; people who dread it are leading tragic lives.
>
> Can you imagine a world in which only a few people were allowed to work? A world in which all the rest of the people were not permitted to do anything useful—all their time had to be spent playing or amusing themselves? Can you imagine the scramble to obtain one of those few jobs that were still available? The privilege of doing useful, necessary work would be recognized as one of the great satisfactions of living.

Being needed—the knowledge that you are doing something useful and necessary—is an essential ingredient of human happiness. Work—done well and to the best of your abilities—is one of the most satisfying of human experiences. What a pity more people don't recognize this!

Why do we lose sight of this fact? Because most of us have to work in order to live. And it rarely occurs to us that something we have to do could actually be enjoyable."

CHAPTER 34

20 FUN GAMES FOR THE OFFICE

"If you want creative workers give them enough time to play.
—*John Cleese, British Actor (1939-present)*

Here is a series of twenty of my favorite games and activities that can be used as ice breakers at your staff meetings or get-togethers. They are fun morale boosters and strong team-builders. And I know you trainers love to find great activities to integrate into your learning programs. It's clear that people learn best when they're having fun.

1. WHO AM I?
Place the name of a famous person on everyone's back. They have to ask questions of each other that can only be answered "yes" or "no" until they find out who they are.

    Elements: Great opening game or warmer upper at a party where people don't know each other.

2. HIT THE PENNY
Two players stand facing each other. A penny is placed on the ground an equal distance between them. The object is to hit the penny with a tennis ball to gain points. But hit the penny carefully so as not to move or push it closer to an opponent, who will then have a better chance to strike it. You score one point for hitting the penny, and five points if it flips over.

    Elements: Great game for the competitive person. Good eye-hand coordination helps.

3. WHEN'S YOUR BIRTHDAY?

Participants set up a row of chairs, one person to a chair. At the signal, people are asked to get up and rearrange themselves in the order of their birthdays. The one whose birthday is closest to January 1st will sit in the first chair and so on down the row, with the person whose birthday is closest to December 31st taking the final seat. The two basic rules of the game are that people are not allowed to talk or write, but they are encouraged to communicate in some way. This is a fun game to watch as the participants negotiate to get to the right seat. Once the group feels they have reassembled correctly, the facilitator goes down the row and asks each person, "When's your birthday?" Anyone out of place is asked to stand while everyone moves over a seat until the standee finds the correct spot. Then the game continues.

Elements: Fun, non-verbal game, perhaps frustrating to some who will feel lost if they can't speak; takes 15 minutes for a group of 20-30 people.

4. YOUR MOST MEMORABLE BIRTHDAY

Participants are asked to pair off. They then interview each other to find out the most memorable birthday experience the other person has had. They are encouraged to be active listeners and to make sure their partner is telling them as complete a story as they can. Once each has told their story to their partner, the facilitator asks a volunteer to share the story that was told to them. Participants are often very eager to tell the other's story, especially if something funny or unique happened on that particular occasion. This is a good way for the group to learn more about each other.

Elements: Verbal and connecting; 10 minutes for the couples to share their stories with each other and another 5 to 10 minutes for individuals to relate others' stories to the whole group.

5. MOST MEMORABLE CHILDHOOD TOY OR GAME

This time participants are encouraged to remember one special toy or game that gave them joy as they were growing up. Once again the leader encourages each "interviewer" to get as complete a story as possible. When all stories are finished, individuals volunteer to tell their partner's tale to the whole group.

6. MATCHING SYMBOLS

Divide the players into groups of four. They form circles and, displaying a clenched fist, declare, "Once, twice, three, *shoot*." At the command of "shoot" they thrust their hands into the middle of the circle. They may keep their hands in the form of a fist or change to a palm facing upwards, a palm facing downwards, or one finger. The object of the game is for every player in the circle to throw out the same symbol at the same time. No talking or planning beforehand is allowed.

Once all groups have been successful at least once, the rules are altered. Now at the command of "shoot," each player is required to throw out a different symbol. That means each group will have a fist, a palm facing upward, a palm facing downward, and a one-finger salute showing.

Elements: This is a fun game and it's great to see the delight and surprise on the faces of participants, either when they match symbols perfectly or fail to do so.

7. KNOTS

This is a game of connection and commitment. Groups of eight arrange themselves into a tightly knit circle, each extending both hands into the middle of the circle. Players now grip each other's hands, literally creating one large knot. Make sure that no one is holding the same two hands of anyone else, or the hand of someone standing right next to them.

Now the game begins. The object is to untie the knot without anyone letting go of another's hand. Participants are encouraged to guide each other along. They realize instinctively that they need to lower or raise their connected hands and arms so that others can step over or slip under. The game is completed when the group finds themselves in one large, unlocked circle. Members do not have to be facing the center. Sometimes the group will find themselves linked in two interlocked or separate circles because of the way they first joined hands. This, too, is a correct way for the game to end.

Depending on the size of the group, the facilitator will have to form several circles, some of which may have more than 8 participants. This is OK but it will challenge the members of those circles a bit more.

Elements: Active; ask pregnant women, people with bad backs, or injured arms or shoulders to sit out. If one circle finishes ahead of the rest of the group, encourage them to reform another "Knot" and start again.

8. YOU CAN'T FOOL US

Participants form two facing lines about 20 feet apart. All the individuals in one of the lines are asked to pick a comfortable pose and then to "freeze." Without any more explanation the opposite line is instructed to turn around so that their backs are facing the first group. Now the true object of the game is revealed. The "posing" line is told that they are about to learn just how observant the members of the other line are. They are directed to rearrange their line so that those standing side by side now switch places with someone else. Also they're encouraged to change their pose. If their hands were in their pockets the first time, it is suggested that they place their hands this time on their hips, behind their backs, etc.

Once line #1 has reconfigured, the second line is invited to turn around. They see that the group they are now facing looks very different. It is their task to undo this new arrangement and return the group to their original positions and their original poses. They can physically move the group around until they are satisfied it is back to its original lineup. Then the first line is asked to report how well line #2 has done. Usually some folks are out of place and feel pleased they have pulled a fast one on the other group.

Then the game starts over, this time with line #2 freezing and line #1 turning their backs while the other group reconfigures. Interestingly, you would think on the second go-around the line that has to reassemble the other group would do it perfectly because they now know the object of the game. But you would be surprised.

The facilitator can "help" make the challenge in the second round more difficult by quietly asking one or two in the posing line to leave the room or to hide in some way, or for a couple of people to switch jackets, sweaters, or other garments.

Elements: Mildly active; 10 to 12 minutes to explain, set up and play two rounds of the game. Leave more time if the two lines are very long.

9. AURA

Stand facing your partner at arm's length. Touch palms together and close your eyes. Feel the energy that you are creating together. Keeping your eyes closed, drop your hands, take two steps backward, and each of you turn around two times. Without opening your eyes, try to relocate your partner by touching your palms together again. There should be no talking or sounds. If the room is filled with people don't be surprised if you end up with a new partner.

You can play an encore version of the game by creating groups of four. Form circles with each of your palms touching the palm of the person to the left and right of you. Then close your eyes, drop palms, take 3 steps backwards this time, turn around two times, and see if your group can get back together.

10. JAN-KEM-PO

This is the Japanese version of the childhood game, "Rocks, Paper, Scissors." The players are divided into groups of 4 or 5. A leader is chosen in each group and makes a fist with his dominant hand. He starts to stroke his fist along his other arm three times, each motion accompanied by the words, "Jan" "Kem" "Po." On the last stroke he shoots out his hand in one of three gestures—a fist for a rock, an open palm to designate paper, or two extended fingers to represent scissors. The other participants shoot out their hands at the same moment with their choice. As with "Rocks, Paper, Scissors," the pecking order is: Rocks smash Scissors, Scissors cuts Paper, and Paper covers Rock. The first participant to beat the leader two times becomes the new leader and the game begins again.

Elements: Safe, opening activity; allow 7-10 minutes so that everyone can be a leader at least once.

11. TELEVISION

This is a more active and visual version of the popular kid's game, "Telephone." In this activity the players form a standing circle. The facilitator is in the middle and explains that when the game begins everyone will have their backs facing the circle. He asks someone to help him demonstrate by assuming this opening position. He walks up to her, taps her on the shoulder, and when she turns around he performs a simple combination movement. They exchange places with the facilitator allowed to face inward. The person who has seen the combination movement now walks up to another person who is helping in the demonstration and whose back is now turned, taps him on the shoulder and performs the exact same combination movement that she originally was shown when he turns around.

Now the actual game begins. The object is to see if the original combination movement can be performed successfully in succession by each member of the group. The fun and surprise is that at some point new movements creep into the original combination. As each player is tapped on the shoulder and turns around, the person doing the tapping and demonstrating the moves switches places and is allowed to watch the changing movements. This continues until all, except one, is facing inward. Then the last person who is tapped observes the movement, steps into the middle of the circle with the facilitator and, at the count of three, both do the motion to see how close it is. Trust me, it won't be close, and people will be stunned and will laugh at the different movements!

Elements: Active; lots of ongoing fun and laughter, particularly when someone observes a combination movement, gets confused, and creates something completely different for the next player. May be played a second time so that people who were tapped towards the end of the game, get tapped earlier in the second go round, and can share the fun that ensues when the movement is changed.

12. STORY CONTINUATION

Groups of 8 to 10 sit in a circle. A person is selected to begin the story. The topic might be, "Once upon a time I came to work and everything had changed." They begin creating a story and the time keeper specifies when time is up (anywhere from 30 to 60 seconds) by saying, "Next" or "Switch." This signals the next person clockwise to use his or her imagination to continue the story where the predecessor left off. The new storyteller must follow the same line of thought when continuing the tale. The game ends when the last person in the circle picks up the story, and completes it in the final 30 to 60 seconds. Of course the last line should always be, "And they lived happily ever after."

Elements: Very verbal, lots of laughs as individuals' creativity and sense of humor show up in the stories.

13. FRUIT BASKET

A large seated circle is created. The facilitator asks each person in turn to declare what their favorite fruit is. The facilitator next explains that she is shopping in a grocery store and selecting an array of fruit she will be serving at a party that everyone has been invited to. She starts naming the different fruit she has selected. At some point she says, "Switch." This is the command for those whose favorite fruit was mentioned to get up and walk to another chair. At the same time the facilitator sits down on an empty chair. Whoever cannot find an empty seat becomes the new shopper. People selecting exotic fruit as their favorite don't realize that they are about to become easy targets for the shopper. During the game the facilitator can add a new rule, explaining that the shopper can begin listing a series of fruit, stop, and declare "fruit basket." Once they do that, every person must get up and change seats. A chaotic scene usually results!

Elements: Very active; make sure pregnant women don't participate, although they should be allowed to sit in the circle; emphasize the need to walk—not run, and make anyone caught running, or body-blocking anyone out of a seat, an instant shopper!

14. A WHAT?

We stand in a circle, facing the center. The facilitator starts the action by placing a soccer ball into the hands of the person on his right, saying, "This is a *banana*." The person now holding the ball is confused because the object certainly does not look like a banana. He inquires back to the leader, "A *What?*" The leader repeats, "A *Banana*!"

Person #2 now hands the Ball to the person on his right and repeats, "This is a *banana*!" #3 is now confused. "A *What?*" she inquires of #2. He turns back to the leader to once again get confirmation, asking, "A *What?*" "A banana!" the leader states again. #2 now turns back to #3 and says, "A banana!" Now that #3 knows what the soccer ball "really" is, she gives the "banana" to #4, says, "This is a banana" and the sequence starts all over again.

At this point the leader takes a different soccer ball, turns to the person on his left, gives it to her and says, "This is a *pineapple*." "A *what?*" says that person and the new sequence, with the "pineapple" begins working itself around the circle clockwise. By the time the two objects cross somewhere in the middle, total confusion will occur. Which is the banana and which is the pineapple? Your guess is as good as mine.

Elements: Lots of fun and laughter in this very silly game; participants will probably be confused at first and the leader should keep reminding them to turn back to the person next to them with the refrain, "A *What?*" Best played when there are more than 15 people participating.

15. NAME RIPPLE

Make sure everyone's name or "nickname" is known. A person selected to start the game calls out one name, adding a physical gesture as they do. Going around the circle clockwise, each person in turn repeats the name and gesture. The action moves around the circle like "a wave" until it gets to the person whose name has been called. That person now announces a new name with a new gesture and the wave or ripple begins anew until it reaches the person who has now been signaled out. Everyone should be named at least once.

16. FACE PASS
Players are arranged in a circle. The presenter creates a strange, distorted face. Once everyone has had a chance to see it, the presenter turns either to his left or right with his frozen face. The second person carefully tries to mirror the expression and then both turn to the center so all can see how successful the attempt has been. The second person now slowly changes her expression until she finds a new one she likes, and then repeats the process by passing her creation to the person next to her. This continues in the same manner around the circle until everyone has had a chance to look totally foolish!

Elements: A very silly but fun game that needs to be played only after people have become comfortable with each other.

17. CONCENTRATION CIRCLE
All players plus one leader stand in a circle and are assigned a number. The leader steps into the middle of the circle and is blindfolded. She is turned around three times. She then calls out one of the numbers. The person whose number has been selected must make his way into the circle, and change places with someone who is at least two to three people away from him, trying to be so quiet that the blindfolded one can't tag or capture him. If player #1 is successful at reaching his goal, the person he is exchanging places with must navigate her way back to the space originally occupied by the first player without being caught. If this happens the person in the middle is informed, and must call out a new number, and the game begins anew. If she tags or captures someone, the blindfold is exchanged and the game starts all over again.

Elements: Active; challenges one's hearing; it's a crowd pleaser; most effective when there are at least 10 people in the circle.

18. PARTNERS
Players choose partners and stand in parallel lines facing each other.

The rule is that one's partner must always answer for the other. You can't answer for yourself. Two people walk up and down the line asking questions of either partner. One of them might say, "When is your birthday?" The partner must come up with an answer. If someone mistakenly answers the question put to them, they must take the place of the questioner.

Elements: Good starting game and getting people into the spirit of fun. Time: 6-8 minutes.

19. TABLEAUS IN MOTION

Groups are formed. They are assigned the same task. It may be to create a movie scene that depicts "Monday morning at your office" or a sports event that captures "how people usually work together." Each group then puts its collective head together and sets the scene, creates the tableau, selects what individual will play what parts, etc. After several minutes of preparation, each group in turn forms their tableau scene, and then put it into motion. At the end of each scene the other groups try to guess what the movie or sports activity is.

Elements: This brings out the budding producers/directors/writers/performers in each group. Usually a lot of humor shows up and there is much laughter; 5-7 minutes to devise the scene, 6-8 minutes for all groups to perform.

20. REVERSE GAUNTLET

The person "running" the gauntlet gets lots of positive attention. Two lines are formed. One person walks or skips between them. She stops at will, faces somebody and looks them in the eye. That person says or does something that makes the gauntlet runner feel good. "I like you," "You are always so positive," "You have the greatest smile," "I can always count on you to help when I'm having a problem at work." Or they can simply hug the person or smile warmly. Then the person "running the gauntlet" moves on to someone else. Each person should approach two different people before someone else assumes the role.

Elements: This activity should continue until everyone has had the chance to "run the gauntlet" two or three times. It's interesting to see how difficult it is for some to accept compliments or praise.

PART SIX

PLAYING ANYTIME, ANYWHERE

CHAPTER 35

GROWNUPS HAVING FUN

"It's a happy talent to know how to play."
—*Ralph Waldo Emerson, American Writer (1803-1882)*

"T-G-I-F, T-G-I-F, Thank God, it's Friday." It's the chant that resounds in many people's heads each Friday morning as they head off for work. But why must we wait until the end of the business week to contemplate all the fun we're going to have on the weekend? We must seize moments in each day to laugh and to play.

Here are a few reports about people, both famous and uncelebrated, who have found ways to play whenever and wherever:

- Emperor Akihito and Empress Michiko of Japan were visiting a nursing home in Tokyo when the Emperor started an impromptu game of "Rock, Paper, Scissors" with an 81-year-old resident. The woman threw out the sign for "Scissors" which beat the Emperor's "Paper." As a penalty for losing he rubbed her shoulders while others in the room clapped and smiled. The massage is one of several traditionally agreed-upon penalties in the game called "Jan-kem-po" that I described in the previous chapter.

- Every November in northeastern Spain, in towns and cities across the Catalonia region, teams of men, women and children climb on each other's shoulders to create human castles. These events are held in town squares and locals and tourists flock to watch them, drawn by the suspense of how many tiers can be built and then dismantled before

169

any spills happen. Performances sometimes last for hours. This tradition dates back as far as the 18th Century.

- United States Senator Hillary Rodham Clinton has some ideas about what constitutes a proper vacation. Once she wrote: "For me, vacations have always meant pulling out the cards, board games and jigsaw puzzles and getting together with family and friends for long relaxing days and evenings of game playing." She says that the former President has a kindred game-playing spirit and that they have spent many hours over the years playing "Trivial Pursuit" and "Charades."

- Douglas Rodriguez, Executive Chef of Ola Restaurant in New York City, once named by *Newsweek* magazine as one of the 100 Americans for the 21st Century, discussed in an article how he approaches food and cooking. "I like to layer flavors and *play* with different textures, to mix something tart with something velvety or buttery, something sweet with something salty, something smooth and something crispy. It is like yin and yang."

- For the last 50-plus years residents of the Spanish city of Bunyol (near Valencia) have celebrated the end of summer by throwing overripe tomatoes at each other. In years past the Bunyolese tossed more than 150,000 lbs. of them.

- Lisa Scheinin is a forensic pathologist for the Los Angeles County coroner's office. She performs between 250 to 300 autopsies a year and, because she is constantly seeing the gruesome side of life—the murders and other violent deaths—she realizes that life is precious and must be lived to the fullest. In a *Los Angeles Times* article she said, "I have to think all the time at work. I don't want to come home and play chess. I want to do something where I can just relax."
For her that means experiencing as many roller coaster rides in a lifetime that she can. She has ridden more than

875 different roller coasters in more than 230 amusement parks around the world. She once rode the Mind Bender, a triple-looping steel coaster in Georgia, 52 times in one day. As she puts it: "I love the whole feel of an amusement park. It's a safe thrill. There's the illusion of danger, but you know nothing's going to happen. It kind of takes me back to being a kid again."

- Joe Lindsay of Pacific Grove, California wrote an indignant letter that the local newspaper, *The Herald*, printed. It said, in part:
  "What happened to honking horns in the Del Monte tunnel? When I was a child growing up here I remember driving through that tunnel with my parents and hearing the many honks of motorists as they zipped along. It seemed playful and fun—a strange thing for adults to be doing. But I remember I liked it, and the sight of mom or dad hitting the horn, laughing and smiling made me feel that maybe they weren't that different from me.
  "When I drive through the tunnel these days I attempt to prime the tunnel with my horn—a few beeps here and there, trying to get back at those memories, but alas, mine is the only horn echoing down that glowing hole. People scowl at me and puzzle at my cheerful face and strange behavior. I am frustrated with people's lack of enthusiasm for this forgotten ritual, but I will continue to lightly honk my horn whenever I go through the tunnel because I feel that it stands for the willingness of an adult to play and be slightly goofy.
  "What happened? Have people just gotten too sullen and serious—too serious to play? Let our honks in the tunnel be that part of ourselves that loves riding bicycles, playing board games and climbing trees. I will keep honking in the tunnel and will be looking forward to the day when I can hear a chorus of horns in there with me."
  Let's hear a honk, honk for Joe! Well said. And when you get home from your drives, Joe, I have a new game waiting for you. I made it up. It should be mandatory for all those

couples who spend most evenings in front of the TV, vying for the clicker, and zapping away. Earlier in the day, begin playing "Hide the Clicker." One of you conceal it in a safe place but do not tell your spouse where it is. Instead, play a game of cards; do a crossword puzzle or cook up a luscious dessert together.

Watching television while holding hands can be a wonderful thing to share but isn't it better sometimes just to turn that "boob tube" off and rediscover why you first fell in love?

CHAPTER 36

THE BEST SURPRISE BIRTHDAY PARTY YOU'LL EVER GIVE

"If you obey all the rules you miss all the fun."
—Katharine Hepburn, Actress (1907-2003)

I have gone to lots of surprise birthday parties in my life including even a few that were thrown for me. And I have often been troubled. Why? The guest of honor always arrives late! According to my logic, that isn't the way it's supposed to be.

Think about it for a moment. A party has been planned for you that you don't know anything about. Most of your friends and family arrive an hour or two before you. They're mingling, having drinks and hors d'oeuvres, and enjoying themselves. In the meantime you've been decoyed. Perhaps your spouse or a friend has told you that they're taking you to dinner or out to drinks. Eventually they do get you to the party. But you've already missed all the arrivals and all the speculation about how surprised (or not surprised) you're going to be. And then you're confronted by 20 or more individuals who all yell "surprise." What pressure! Now you have to deal with lots of smiling people wanting your attention. It is overwhelming!

Well I have an alternative suggestion that I think makes more sense. Go ahead and plan that surprise party for your mate or your parent or a friend. Have a great time organizing it. Enlist other friends or family members. Pick a date. Pick a spot. And then on that special day take the honored guest to the location before anyone else shows up. Just as in a traditional surprise party, use an excuse to lure him to the place. And when he arrives and sees all the decorations and perhaps the caterers and the hired bartenders and servers, explain to him what's up.

"Oh we're having a surprise birthday party for you."

When he or she appears stunned and mystified and unbelieving, just explain that everyone has been in on the secret and is so excited. Don't answer any more of her questions. Tell her to get a drink and relax and get ready for the party that's about to start. In the meantime you have organized the guests to come at different time intervals. Soon the first folks show up. The honoree is already there! She gets a chance to greet everyone as they arrive. She gets to say how surprised she is. She experiences it over and over again as new friends and family join the group. She has truly been surprised and yet is at the party from the beginning—mingling, eating, drinking, and fully enjoying her special occasion. Try it – you'll like it. And so will the guest of honor!

CHAPTER 37

AN INVITATION TO AN "ADULTS ONLY" PARTY

"What makes me happy is playing games. That's what I like to do."

That's Barbara Dreyfuss speaking. She's a friend of mine and a former director of administration for a high-pressured Los Angeles public relations firm. Barbara's referring specifically to board games and says that her all-time favorite has always been "Monopoly," which she used to play as a youth and teen with her very competitive brother. He always won but this did not deter her in any way. So, many years later she decided to translate this love of hers into a grownups-only games party. "I thought I would generate some excitement and enthusiasm by doing something in the way of a fun invitation in an environment that was conducive to playing games."

The first step for her was the invitation—and she knew instinctively what that would be. She had been experimenting with computers and utilized her newly learned skills to create an imitation "Monopoly" game board. Where the different streets and properties traditionally are, she substituted her own messages. Right after GO was the word "fun" with the explanation, "play games, swim, sun, eat and drink." In another box the word "when" replaced the property name and announced the date and time. A corner box warned, "Penalty for not bringing your suits, towels, and lotions." Along the board "Poker," "Trivial Pursuit," "Chess," "Dominos," "Cribbage" and other games were listed.

She knew that she wanted to make it an annual event, provide lots of food, have it set around her condo pool, and include all her close friends (who certainly knew of her love for games), but also many of her business associates. She hoped that everyone would want to play. She even provided sign-up sheets to get the ball rolling, but was also sensitive to those she thought would rather sit and do nothing. So, one of the sheets was labeled, "just going to sit there." The first party was a great success. I was there and I told all my friends about it for weeks afterwards. Meanwhile Barbara was beginning to think about her next year's invitation.

This time she wanted the invite to be delivered in a can of "Pickup Sticks"—an artifact from another fun game she played as a child. She envisioned each invitee receiving an individual tin in the mail, opening it and dumping out the wooden sticks, with the invitation falling out as well. But she soon learned that the original ones weren't made anymore. The new version of the game utilizes plastic sticks that come apart, and they're not packaged in a tube like the original ones were. Barbara was bummed!

She thought about it for awhile and finally came up with an alternative plan. She found a small inexpensive checkerboard that was packaged with a set of red and black checkers. This she decided would serve as the invitation. But then she discovered that the envelopes she had already purchased were too small. She finally figured her way around that, but then another problem cropped up. This new predicament, however, ended up being a lot of fun rather than an annoyance.

"When I realized the invitation was going to need special postage because of the size I really fretted because I wanted to carry the whole theme out. I like movies an awful lot and had already purchased the beautiful commemorative Alfred Hitchcock stamps, the denomination of which were now insufficient, so I went back to the post office to see what my options were. When they told me that among the 3-cent stamps the choices were birds I knew they were the ones I wanted. So it ended up being fun for me. I had to put five of them on each envelope. I laughed every time I put a stamp on! And though very few people realized the significance of the bird stamps surrounding the Alfred Hitchcock stamp it didn't matter because I had so much fun. It's all play for me and it keeps me young, more alert, more in tune with a lot of things.

"For exercise I walk up and down the stairs every day. I think about exercise but that doesn't excite me the way playing a game does. It doesn't make me smile; it doesn't make me think I'm challenging my mind. And it's important for me to keep mentally alert and game playing gives me that opportunity. It makes me feel great!"

I, along with everyone else, always had fun at Barb's game parties. I even met my mate at the last party she threw, which was more than five years ago. I miss them a lot. Barbara it's time to put your planning hat back on. We want to party again!

CHAPTER 38

XMAS TREE XTRAVAGANZAS

"There's nothing sadder in this world than to awake Christmas morning and not be a child."
—Erma Bombeck, American Humorist (1927-1996)

Steve and Sasha are two adults who know how to play *big time*! Their home is filled with loads of toys and other fun objects. In talking with each of them you immediately get a sense of two very playful people.

Sasha grew up in New York. Her parents used to take her to see the Roller Derby. Then she and all the neighborhood kids would take to the streets, re-enacting the "drama" they had witnessed. They would clamp their roller skates onto their shoes, split up into teams, and race around an oval that they had drawn on the ground with chalk. It was great fun.

Steve was into "his drama" too. It was called "Army." Every day the kids would rush outside with their toy rifles and their army fatigues and stage make-believe wars. One day the game changed. Someone's parents weren't home and the game became "Army/Storm the Fort." He found that infinitely better. One team would hide in the house while the other team tried "to take it." Steve swears that they never did any damage to the inside of the house and the parents never found out what was going on. He got a special kick out of that game because it was a little "forbidden."

The "drama" continues for them as adults but it's on a whole different level now. And because I believe it's quite a unique and wonderful form of play, I wanted to share it with you. For over 20 years they've hosted a very special Christmas party that none of their friends or business associates would dare to miss. Why? All year long they've been wondering and anticipating what Steve and Sasha's Christmas tree will look like.

Every December Steve and Sasha create a delightfully playful version of this ultimate Christmas symbol. It started as a joke—a commentary on the utter commercialism of the season—but has now grown into a unique art form.

It first took shape in San Francisco in late 1981 after they had moved in together. Sasha wanted to have a tree but Steve did not. Being Jewish he had never had one growing up. But Sasha, who is Jewish as well, had always had one for her young daughter Ilena, who is half-Catholic. The disagreement escalated. Then one day while Sasha and her daughter were out, Steve had a wild flash.

He went downstairs and grabbed the bicycle that was stored by the front door, brought it upstairs, and began to tinker with it. He turned the front wheel perpendicular to the rest of the bike, fastened it with some wire, and stood it up on end. When Sasha and Ilena returned to find the standing bicycle in the corner they were perplexed. Steve offered his vision to them.

"That's our Christmas tree. We'll decorate this."

"Wow, cool, okay that's fine," was their instant response.

The "bicycle tree" took on a life of its own. As Steve explains: "It was a solution to the problem and it was a fun and idiosyncratic little artful project that we could all get involved with. We thought it was such a cool thing and so tacky. What a tacky thing! It had lights and ornaments, and a star on top. We put some presents around it and thought it was the funniest thing we had ever seen. So we decided to have a party. We sent out invitations to all our friends and they all came. People loved it. It was funny. They got the humor behind it. It wasn't anti-religious. We were doing something that was more anti-commercial which most of our friends could get behind."

A year later they started thinking about creating a novel tree again. During one of the discussions they noticed the coat rack standing in the corner. "We can make a tree out of that," they exclaimed almost in unison. And they did, and had another party as well. That "tree" even got some local publicity. Steve was working at television station KPIX in San Francisco at the time. A co-worker took pictures of it and it was featured on a newscast.

The tradition was reborn once they moved to Los Angeles. They had made lots of new friends and decided to treat them to their unique form of play. Earlier that year their TV antenna had blown off the roof and Steve had stored it in the garage rather than throwing it away. When Christmas came around and they thought about "the tree," he said, "Why don't we just decorate that?"

Creativity was the watchword in 1988. In their discussions they noted how people always decorate Christmas trees with all those little balls on it. So they posed this idea: "Why don't we get a huge ball and decorate it with little Christmas trees." Steve describes what they came up with: "It was a paper-mache ball that stood four or five feet tall. We built it in the garage in two pieces so that we could fit it in the door into our house, and then we assembled it in the living room. We built it together. It was a lot of fun because it was our project."

Sasha notes how the labor is divided. "Steve is in charge of the construction. I'm the artist." And indeed she is. As a young person she studied drawing and painting and eventually had a studio of her own. Her work was exhibited in galleries both here in the United States and abroad. Steve happens to have a degree in architecture although he has never worked in that field professionally. The designing and building elements usually fall to him.

Through the years Steve and Sasha have taken photos of all their trees. It sits in a large picture frame, which is exhibited next to each year's new tree so that people can reminisce over past "masterpieces."

"We'll meet new people from work and include them in the next year's party and they'll come in and stand by the pictures of all the trees and go 'wow' and someone will come up proudly saying, 'You know I've been coming to this party since *that* tree.'"

When I saw the photo of the tree from 1993 I began to laugh. Steve explained why they had stacked bags of steer manure together to form the tree: "I think that was my first year as a salesperson for a large company and I realized the great amounts of bullshit that permeated every day. So I said, 'let's make a tree out of bullshit.' I went to Bandini and actually bought empty bags at 50 cents apiece. They were clean bags and I went to a packaging store and bought popcorn. But I had a disagreement with Sasha. I wanted to take a cup of fertilizer and hide it in the tree so that you could at least get the essence of it. She said 'I don't want that in the house' and I said okay."

When Steve discusses the 1996 tree he becomes animated as he recalls his favorite creation of all, and the one that he feels is superior to anything else that has been done. "It is a send-up of the air fresheners that are used in cars, the ones that are shaped like a tree. It is a royal pine car freshener. It is done to scale exactly and it's 6 feet tall. The fun part about it is that there's a mirror mounted on the ceiling and the tree actually hangs from it with no support underneath. It's suspended from the mirror."

Why does Steve like creating and making these Christmas trees every year?

"It's a form of the way I play. I don't go out and play with toy dinosaurs anymore but when I'm building something like this, that's an expression of play because I'm building something that's whimsical and I am enjoying the craft of it."

For 1997 their surprise tree was perhaps the greatest one of all. "It was driven by the fact that we only had a small space in the corner to decorate and all the ideas we had in reserve at the time were not going to work," Steve recalls. As he was shaving one morning he came up with the idea. "Why don't we put it on the ceiling?" He conceptualized stringing wires between all the walls to create the form of a Christmas tree that would hang as a canopy over everyone's head. He went and told Sasha and her response was, "That's it. It's perfect!"

"The fun thing is people walked into the room and didn't know where the tree was. Sasha and I had people come up to us and say, 'Where's the tree?' I would just point up and they would look up and go, 'Oh my God!' I loved that they didn't see it. That was fun, watching people go through the realization that the tree was above them."

All the ornaments were suspended from the tree. And by now Steve and Sasha have lots of them. That's because their guests get to "play" also by participating in a "Tacky Christmas Ornament Contest." This has become an integral part of their holiday party, and their friends are always encouraged to make their ornament themselves or take some time to find something strange and different.

So, after so many years of trees, is the fun wearing thin? "No way," says Steve. "I like finishing it, presenting it, looking at it, admiring it and having other people come together to enjoy it. The frustrating feelings are always very fleeting and the feeling is a sense of accomplishment, a sense of realizing some artistic vision."

CHAPTER 39

FANTASY BASEBALL FOR FUN AND PROFIT

> "The game begins in the spring when everything else begins again, and it blossoms in the summer, filling the afternoons and evenings, and then as soon as the chill rains come, it stops and leaves you to face the fall alone."
> —A. Bartlett Giamatti, Commissioner of Baseball (1938-1989)

Over seven million Americans participate in a game called Fantasy Baseball. I am one of them. For many years I have looked forward to the start of baseball's new season and anticipated the fun I will have creating my own fantasy team and watching its progress throughout the season.

The original concept began about 25 years ago when a New York writer joined other like-minded fans to form a league of their own, which they called the "Rotisserie League Baseball Association." Named for the now defunct "Le Rotisserie" French restaurant in New York where they often met, the group created the initial idea of simulating the owning and managing of their very own baseball team. The participants selected actual baseball players from the major leagues and followed their batting and pitching statistics through the season. The winner got a cash award and a trophy.

Our league was created soon after, here on the West Coast, as a variation on that original rotisserie game theme. It was launched by a friend, Bill Lustig, who believed that several of his buddies might be interested. That first year Bill and I, along with original owners Frank Bigelow, John Castor, Jeff Jaffee, Lloyd Kajikawa, Richard Molander, (we are still active players) and some others who eventually lost interest, met to discuss our new plaything and to create the rules.

A few years ago we even created a trophy which goes to the guy whose team comes in first. The winner gets to take it home and show it off to his friends until the following year when the next champion has his name engraved on it and takes possession. It is named in memory of two former owners, Richard Marion and Bob Becker, who both died much too young.

Our ten team league is currently composed of an educator, a realtor, four attorneys, a travel executive, four fellows who work in the film business, and me, the motivational speaker. Because all of us have stressful lives, we look forward to escaping into our little game of make-believe, contemplating what players we will trade for or draft each year, and how we can outwit our fellow players to finish at the top of the heap.

Jeff Jaffee, whom we have affectionately dubbed "Mr. Baseball," plays our fantasy game as well as anyone. He first started following real baseball when he was just five years old. As he recalls, "Being from New York in the early 50s there were three teams and you loved one and hated the other two. That was true of most New Yorkers. I loved the Dodgers and bitterly hated the Giants and Yankees—still do."

And he has no doubt that this intense interest in our Fantasy Baseball league has its origins in his youth. "When I was a kid, basically all I thought was about baseball. I constantly played it, threw a ball off the roof, off the stoop, off my brother! A friend and I used to play stickball and we would actually go through the line-ups of our teams, me being a Dodger fan and he being a Yankee fan and, if a lefty hitter came up, we hit lefty and a right hitter came up we hit righty, so we actually became the players. We tried to use their stance and that added to the fun of the whole experience. And we used to announce the games. That was a very important part of it. (Affecting an echo) Now, now, batting, num, num, ber, ber, eight, Yogi, Yogi, Berra, Berra."

But it wasn't just the playing of those simulated games that today connects him so strongly with his love for Fantasy Baseball. It's something else: "I used to play various board games also and kept copious statistics of every move of my Dodgers against every other team. One was called *Red Barber's All Star Baseball* which was a board, dice game. This was the game I used to keep my statistics on. I had books full of statistics of each game, each at bat."

The three teams that finish at the top of our league each year receive a cash award besides the trophy. Jeff almost always grabs one of those positions. "I like to win and I try to win every single year. I do everything I can to win. Important to win? Not really. It's playing the game."

And that's perhaps why Jeff is so good at this game. He approaches it as a form of play. In fact it goes ever deeper. "I think that my whole life has been play. When I was in the middle of my college years I looked at people and said I don't understand why people work until they're 65 and then retire. I'm going to retire and then I'll worry about what I'm going to do when I'm 65. So basically the first thing I did when I graduated from law school was to become a candle maker." Jeff never did practice law. Eventually he gravitated to the film and TV business and for the last 18 years has secured "props" for movies, commercials, and television series. Why has that job been so satisfying for him?

"Props are the only area that changes constantly. It's like a scavenger hunt. It is a game, a form of play. You basically have to find, invent, rent, make, and put together a hundred elements until it's time to shoot."

Jeff once did fantasize trying to look for a career in the baseball world. He believes he would have been a terrific general manager for a major league team. But for now, our fantasy baseball bet will have to do.

And it can be a source of great fun for you too. There are countless books on the subject. Many newspapers, sports networks, and sports Internet sites host Fantasy Baseball leagues every year. So if you want a playful adventure and a chance to once more live the baseball dreams of your childhood, seek out fantasy baseball. I know you'll write and thank me if you do.

CHAPTER 40

HOW MUCH DO YOU BID FOR THIS DESSERT?

"Games lubricate the body and the mind."
—Benjamin Franklin, American Statesman
(1706-1790)

Do you want to throw a party that's really different? Try one of my Mystery Dessert Parties. Invite folks who you know are fun to be with and have a spirit of creativity and play. Explain to them that everyone attending must show up with a dessert (either store bought or homemade), concealed in a closed box or package so that the other guests don't know what you've brought. Limit the cost of the dessert to not more than say five to six dollars.

As the attendees get there collect the mystery desserts and ask whether any have to be refrigerated. Then organize some games, maybe "Charades" or "Dictionary." Spend a few hours playing with your friends.

Now it's time for "The Dessert Game." Prepare some coffee or tea and have each person place their concealed dessert on their lap. Draw lots to see who will go first, second, and so on when selection time comes. But first have each person in turn give a brief hint of what they have on their lap, but not reveal the actual contents. The idea is to "sell" your dessert. Person #1 might say: "My dessert is a form of pastry. It is very sweet and has a fruit element incorporated in it. If you like cakes or pies you will love this offering."

The person next to them clockwise around the circle presents her offering: "My dessert cannot be classified as a pastry. But if you like chocolate you probably are going to want to select it. I don't think you have ever eaten anything as good as this."

Then it's time for the next person to spin a short tale about their distinctive treat. Once everyone has had a turn it's selection time. Whoever drew lot number one goes first and can select the dessert on anyone's lap, giving his to them in return. Or, he can choose to keep his own. Number two goes next. She can select what number one has just picked, or any other dessert, or keep her own. We go around the circle until everyone has had a chance to make a selection. But we're not through yet!

The host now asks if everyone is happy with the still mysterious dessert they've selected. This is where the fine-tuning comes in. If someone intuitively wants to switch, they can ask the person who has the dessert box that they now desire whether they will exchange boxes. If the answer is "yes" then the switch is made. Or three people can get together and make a triple switch. Person number three gives the dessert they now have to number five who in turn gives their dessert to number seven. Then number seven gives the dessert on their lap to number three.

Finally everyone gets to open the box or package now on their lap, see what they have selected, and start eating. Every single time I have organized this game everyone ends up sharing their dessert with everyone else. If that isn't community then what is?

CHAPTER 41

52 WEEKS OF PLAY IDEAS

> "We live to play—that is my slogan, under which we shall set about the real things of life, and be as busy, and in the same spirit, as is nature on a morning in Spring."
> —William Butler Yeats, Irish Poet (1865-1939)

Here's a chance for you to use some of your creativity to plan a play-happening for every week of the year. Below are themes and suggestions coinciding with holidays, events, and different key periods from the beginning of January to the end of December.

What will be your take on Thanksgiving and Christmas this year? How about Valentine's Day and St. Patrick's Day next year? What kind of "football hi-jinks" are you going to plan at the end of January, and what might your "Color War" look like in June? Do you have any novel party ideas for the World Series, the Grammy and Academy Awards®, and some fun events you could organize during tax season and the beginning of Spring? Does "turning over a new leaf" in January involve going to see a psychic who reads tea leaves?

Instructions on how to organize a "Mystery Dessert Party" and rules for playing the game, "Hit the Penny," are found elsewhere in the book. But most of the great ideas for celebrating will come from your fertile imagination. Will you be taking a whirlwind trip to Punxsutawney, Pennsylvania to see groundhog Phil emerge from his cave during the first week in February? Or, instead, will you rent the entertaining Bill Murray film, *Groundhog Day*, and plan a potluck with some of your friends? Why not vow to go on an amusement park ride that really scares you during the fourth week in May. Make sure you take a photograph to show everyone how brave you really are. So go ahead—start planning!

JANUARY
WK. 1 NEW YEAR'S—TURNING OVER A NEW LEAF
WK. 2 BOOK DISCUSSION WITH HOT CHOCOLATE
WK. 3 GAME NIGHT—JIGSAW PUZZLES, CHARADES
WK. 4 SUPER BOWL FOOTBALL HI-JINKS

FEBRUARY
WK. 1 GROUNDHOG GRAZING—TRIP TO THE ZOO
WK. 2 VALENTINE'S DAY IS NOT JUST FOR LOVERS
WK. 3 WASHINGTON'S BIRTHDAY CHERRY PIE JUBILEE
WK. 4 ACADEMY AWARDS® PARTY WITH COSTUME

MARCH
WK. 1 GRAMMYS ROCK 'N' ROLL PARTY
WK. 2 BASEBALL APPROACHES: CREATE A FANTASY LEAGUE
WK. 3 ST. PATRICK'S DAY LEPRECHAUNS
WK. 4 "MARCH MADNESS": BASKETBALL SHOOTING CONTEST
WK. 5 ARBOR DAY—NATURE WALK BLINDFOLDED

APRIL
WK. 1 APRIL FOOL'S DAY—PRACTICAL JOKE PARTY
WK. 2 TAX TIME – "HIT THE PENNY" COMPETITION
WK. 3 PLAYING AT THE OFFICE: BRING A NEW TOY TO WORK
WK. 4 SPLISH, SPLASH—PLAYING OUTSIDE IN THE RAIN

MAY
WK. 1 MAY DAY AROUND THE FLAG POLE
WK. 2 MOTHER'S DAY—"MOTHER MAY I?"
WK. 3 LET'S GO TO THE MOVIES—NEW SUMMER RELEASES
WK. 4 AMUSEMENT PARK MAYHEM
WK. 5 MEMORIAL DAY PICNIC

JUNE
WK. 1 MINIATURE GOLF
WK. 2 FLAG DAY COLOR WAR
WK. 3 LET'S GET MARRIED "AGAIN" CELEBRATION
WK. 4 IT'S PARACHUTE PLAY FOR ADULTS TIME

JULY
WK. 1 4TH OF JULY PATRIOTISM
WK. 2 MYSTERY BUS TOUR
WK. 3 FATHER'S DAY COOK-OUT AND HORSESHOE PITCHING
WK. 4 SPLISH, SPLASH PARTY

AUGUST
WK. 1 BARBECUE AND BEACH BALL BONANZA
WK. 2 LUAU ON THE SAND
WK. 3 SECRET WEEKEND GETAWAY TRIP
WK. 4 LATE SUMMER PROGRESSIVE DINNER PARTY

SEPTEMBER
WK. 1 LABOR DAY BOXED GAMES GET TOGETHER
WK. 2 HOORAY THE KIDS ARE BACK IN SCHOOL PARTY
WK. 3 FOOTBALL RETURNS—TABLE FOOTBALL
WK. 4 MYSTERY DESSERT PARTY

OCTOBER
WK. 1 HOCKEY BEGINS—ICE SKATING PARTY
WK. 2 COLUMBUS DAY EXPEDITION TO THE MUSEUM
WK. 3 HAUNTED HOUSE VISIT
WK. 4 SEANCE
WK. 5 HALLOWEEN PARTY—BOBBING FOR APPLES

NOVEMBER
WK. 1 ELECTION DAY PIN THE TAIL ON THE POLITICIAN
WK. 2 COLLEGE BASKETBALL TIPOFF
WK. 3 MENU SWAPPING IN PREPARATION FOR THE HOLIDAYS

WK. 4   TURKEY RUN

DECEMBER
WK. 1   XMAS TREE XTRAVAGANZAS
WK. 2   HANUKAH, KWANZAA TREATS
WK. 3   HOLIDAY GIFT-WRAPPING PARTY
WK. 4   CHRISTMAS CHEER
WK. 5   NEW YEAR'S FROLIC

PART 7
CELEBRITY CHILDHOODS

CHAPTER 42

TOM HANKS WAS ONCE A KID TOO!

"A musician must make music, an artist must paint, a poet must write if he is to be ultimately at peace with himself. What one can be, one must be."
—Abraham Maslow, American Psychologist (1908-1970)

Often, critics feel that actors and actresses are just grownup children, using their career as a way to play even more. What's wrong with that? During my years in show business I always admired the way performers brought a sense of fun and play into their work. The late, wonderful star of television's *Saturday Night Live*, Gilda Radner, once said: "Genius is the ability to recapture one's childhood at will."

In researching this book I came across quotes from several celebrated actors, actresses and athletes who revealed how their childhoods prepared them for their careers. Also some good lessons they've learned during the course of their lives. Here are just a few examples.

TOM HANKS
As a child growing up in Concord, California, he used to imagine being the kind of astronaut he later would play in *Apollo 13*, Jim Lovell. Hanks said he "would put a brick in the bottom of my pants and sit at the bottom of the pool breathing through a garden hose and kind of, like, float." Also he used to "take apart the pool ladder and put it back together again, because I wanted to be doing a service in zero gravity of outer space."

Hanks recalls that he also liked to play with dolls—astronaut dolls, that is. One of them was named "Major Matt Mason," and he remembers playing with that particular toy at "the coffee table in my mom's living room for hours and hours."

MEGAN MULLALY
Last year Megan, one of the co-stars of NBC's *Will & Grace*, tripped on the stairs while going onstage to accept her Screen Actors Guild trophy for best comedy series actress. Backstage, she said it was not her fault, blaming another famous actress for what happened:
    "I tripped up the stairs trying to tell Meryl Streep that I love her," said Mullally, who has now won the award three-years running. "I was mouthing 'I love you,' and then I fell down." As to why SAG voters have selected her and co-star and fellow actor winner Sean Hayes several times, Mullally said: "I think it's because the characters are both very childlike. It's a really appealing quality, and it appeals to everyone. It's nice to be able to let go and be a kid again."

KEVIN BACON
He grew up in Philadelphia, the youngest of six kids. Both parents encouraged a love of art and music. According to him, "There were lots of instruments in the house. We were always dancing. And I had a big box of old clothes that were my favorite toys as a kid. I loved playing dress-up."
    His mother encouraged Kevin to take acting classes. He moved to New York City to study at the Circle in the Square Theatre when he was only 17. "I was driven," he says. "Even as a kid, I definitely had my eyes on the prize."

LILY TOMLIN
Speaking of the revival of her successful theatre project, *The Search for Signs of Intelligent Life in the Universe*, she finds it to be exhilarating. "It's such a joy to perform. As I've lived longer, I've grown in touch with my joy—I keep using that word, but I can't think of a better way to describe it. It's fun to play, you know."

TIGER WOODS
Already one of the greatest golfers that the world has ever seen, Tiger Woods continues to amaze us with his natural ability and talent. Once, playing in a tournament in Thailand, he said: "Always keep the game fun. Obviously golf is a very serious part of my life, but when you stop having fun at it, that's when it's time to hang it up."

ELAINE STRITCH
This musical comedy star and actress who won a Tony Award for her sensational one woman show kicked off the National Council on Alcoholism and Drug Dependence lunch with these words: "I don't think my Broadway show would have been a hit without booze. I had a lot of fun drinking in my time. But the joy of living free, and the discipline of not drinking, is beginning to be my addiction.

"'Joy' is my favorite word in the English language, and I never felt joy when I was drinking. Now I actually find myself going along sometimes and skipping, just like a child."

BRITNEY SPEARS
Last year, after wrapping up her international performing tour in Mexico City—where she had to cut her concert short because of bad weather and some bad press for flashing a finger at photographers outside an airport—she explained to *People* magazine in a cover story: "I'm taking a break, so people are writing that I'm having a meltdown. I don't get it. I need this break to rejuvenate and to just play."

CHAPTER 43

MARVIN HAMLISCH HAD A TRAIN SET

"We are most nearly ourselves when we achieve the seriousness of the child at play."
—*Heraclitus, Greek Philosopher (late 6th Century B.C.)*

When noted composer and Academy Award®-winner Marvin Hamlisch was growing up, his parents, his sister and he lived in a small one-bedroom apartment in New York City's borough of Manhattan. What he remembers most vividly is his early fascination with toy cars and trains.

"I used to get these cars as gifts and they'd be so much fun. I remember one car specifically and I remember how I got it! My parents and my sister always went to Chicago to visit our cousins every Passover. I had small little inky dinky cars but my cousin had a fabulous red car. And you know how it is. His mother says to him, 'Give Marvin the red car because he came all the way from New York,' and he did, screaming all the way."

Because of that yearly trip to Chicago, which was made by train, Marvin also became totally consumed by this mode of travel. When he was about nine he convinced his father to buy him a train set. Marvin recalls the trip into Manhattan to make the purchase.

"Since I was five years old we had always taken the train to Chicago so I had in my mind the word 'Super Chief.' American Flyer made such a train. It was six-and-a-half-feet long. I'll never forget it. It had domed cars that lit up and my father obviously could not afford this train because it was very expensive. But there was another train that was cheaper and he kept pushing me to get that train. So they put this train on the tracks to let me see how it was going to go around, and I remember it went around once and then it fell over. And I looked at my father with the brain of a nine-year-old saying, 'This wouldn't happen with the Super Chief,' and my poor father who was such a sweet man, bought that Super Chief, which probably meant that he couldn't buy himself a coat or underwear for the next six months!"

When they got the train set home to their small apartment, Marvin's father had the tracks screwed into a board so it would be ready to use whenever Marvin wanted to play with his trains. All he had to do was pull the board out from behind the upright piano in the living room where Marvin slept and set up his trains. That happened most often during Christmas vacation.

"I not only set up the train set but here's the lunacy. I would go to Grand Central Station and get the actual time table of a train that went from New York to Chicago. Because I had gone to Chicago so many times I knew it was an 18-hour trip. Usually it left about 5:00 or 6:00 in the evening. I know you're not going to believe this but I would then run my trains exactly to the times! But it got worse than that.

"Let's say it was going to get into Pittsburgh at 11:27. I would have an alarm clock. My mother is sleeping, my father is sleeping, my sister is sleeping and I'm trying to sleep, and there's a train running in the living room around this couch where I slept. So at 11:25 I would wake up and call Grand Central Station to find out if the train was running on time. They'd say the train is 18 minutes late. So I would stay up another 18 minutes and I'd slow the train down and literally stop it until the time it was supposed to arrive. The next place was Cleveland, 3:30 am. I would set the alarm clock for 3:20.

"Now let me tell you what a great mother I had. Normal mothers would say, 'You've now gone insane. Let me get you a pill. We can deal with this.' However my mother said, 'Is there anything you want to eat? Do you want a tuna fish sandwich because you're going to be up at 3:30?' And at 3:25 I would call Grand Central Station. 'Hello is the train on time? No?' Usually those trains were always late. Train's now 40 minutes late. My mother would get up. She'd make me tea with milk and feed me Social Tea Biscuits which I loved, and there I was as a kid in my pajamas at 3:30 in the morning with my train set. I literally stayed up all during my Christmas vacation."

Marvin has a poignant follow-up to this childhood memory. "When I was in my 20s I said to my father, 'You know, Daddy, I love my train so much and I want to take it to my house on Long Island. Would you pack it for me?' because I knew if he packed it, it would be forever packed right. He had been an accordionist and so he packed it inside one of his old accordion cases.

"All of a sudden several years ago it came upon me that I wanted to get back the feeling of family. So I went to the garage and got the suitcase that my father had used to pack the train set. I still had the board. Do you know I set up my train set for the first time since I was a child and it was so meaningful because it brought back the whole sense of being safe at home. Your parents are there to take care of you and if you want to run the set at 2:30 in the morning it's okay."

CHAPTER 44

HIDING OUT WITH SUZANNE SOMERS

"It isn't where you came from, it's where you're going that counts."
—*Ella Fitzgerald, American Singer (1917-1996)*

The noted actress, author and entrepreneur Suzanne Somers has been quite open about her struggles growing up in an alcoholic family. In her best-selling book, *Keeping Secrets,* Suzanne revealed how her mother and siblings were ruled by her alcoholic father's abusive behavior and drunken rages. In the book she recalls that:

> "He would throw things around the house, dishes would break and doors would slam. He'd stumble and fall and swear. The noise was frightening. I'd lie in my room and tremble."

Eventually her mother created a place for the family to hide when her father was in one of his drunken states. They climbed into her Brother Danny's closet. She remembers that it had a latch on the inside so they could lock themselves in—her mother, brother and sister huddling together as her father created havoc downstairs. Feeling closed in and safe, and having a place to hide, eventually became one of the important ways she chose to play.

"When I think about how I played as a kid a lot of it was solitary, a lot of it was in my room. I would make forts and crawl inside the forts by pulling chairs and pieces of furniture together and putting blankets over the top."

And what was one of her favorite play things?

"Paper dolls—I guess I loved clothes and fashion, because I would draw little shirts and little skirts and little shoes and then make tabs to fold them back on my main doll and I would create friends. These dolls were friends. I had one doll who was a nurse and another doll who was a fashion model. These were the friends I had that I played with."

There was a good reason why she picked that nurse doll and why one of her first fantasies growing up was to one day become a nurse.

"The nature of a child in an alcoholic family is that you take on different roles and I took care of everybody or I thought I was. In my own mind this whole family was either surviving or falling apart as a result of my actions. It was a lot of responsibility that I took on myself. But a nurse was perfect because she could help everybody."

Remembering from my own childhood that some of the little girls in my neighborhood played with paper dolls too—often modeled after actresses of the time—I asked Suzanne if she ever had one of those sets. Her response made me laugh.

"If there had been any doll it would have been Debbie Reynolds because my dream as a child would be that Debbie Reynolds and Eddie Fisher would have car trouble in front of my house and have to come in and they'd eat dinner with us and they'd like me so much that they took me home with them. That was my big fantasy. So a lot of my fantasy, because of the nature of my childhood, and a lot of my play was escape. Making these dolls took me into another world and gave me the kind of clothes for them to wear that we couldn't afford as a family. I had forgotten about my dolls—I loved them."

Suzanne has always been a glamorous figure but I wanted to know if she ever had a time in her childhood when she played as a tomboy.

"No. I was always a girly-girl. I loved my dresses. I couldn't wait to wear my sister's high heels. In fact, from the time I was 9 years old, the moment she would leave the house I'd have the high heels on and I had her bras on and I'd stuff them with Kleenex.

I remember Sandy my girlfriend and I went to San Francisco and we snuck my sister's high heels and bras and, when we got off the bus we went into the bathroom and put on the heels and bras and stuffed them with the Kleenex and then we went to see Santa Claus. Two little 10-year-old girls in high heels and big old boobs."

It's interesting that none of her early play ever had anything to do with show business and she never ever fantasized being a performer when she grew up. There was a reason.

"My sister was being groomed to be the performer. My mother played piano for the dance lessons so I would go with her. I was only 4 years old, and I would just sit and watch and eventually I got to take tap for a couple of years but it was never serious, and I wasn't the one who was going to be the performer. My sister was a natural—she was more flamboyant, and more outgoing, and better looking, and everything."

What she thought she *could* do was to one day be a good cook. "There was a book called *Suzy's Cookbook*. My mother would read me that at night—it was the only book I wanted her to read. It had recipes. One was a for candle salad. You take a piece of lettuce, then you take a pineapple slice and put it on top of the piece of lettuce and then you take a scoop of cottage cheese and put it in the center of the pineapple and then you cut a banana half and put it inside the cottage cheese which holds it straight up like glue. Then you put a maraschino cherry on the top, and that's the candle salad.

"But to me as a little girl, the first time I heard that I realized, 'I could do that, I could do that!' So it kept reinforcing that and she read that book to me over and over until she couldn't stand it. But it made me feel smart because I knew what was coming next. 'Yes then you put the cottage cheese right, then you cut the banana in half and put it in.'

"And the other thing I had as a child was a little electric stove. It looked like a stove but probably was a concept of a heating pad. I could cook on it and I could make little cakes in the little oven and things I cooked on the top and that fascinated me."

Is it any wonder that Suzanne is still involved with food and its preparation and has made a major success for herself? More than two million people have discovered her Somersize program, a concept for eating great foods while losing weight at the same time. Through her four books and her personal products—from candy to BBQ sauce and ketchup—she has become quite the entrepreneur.

But her food preparation still remains "play" for her. When we talked she told me how she had spent the previous days: "What I did to wind down was to cook all weekend. I made homemade tomato soup and I made things that needed a lot of long slow cooking, a lot of patience, tasting, adding, and I was mesmerized by it. And Saturday night I had a couple of friends over for dinner and one said, 'I can't believe you. You work all week and you cook all day' and I think, you don't understand this is how I wind down. Total balance. So I'm still cooking. I'm the only headliner in Vegas with dish-pan hands!"

Suzanne also has five grandchildren whom she adores, and I was curious to know how she plays with them. "We write books together and we do makeup. We look at my Suzanne Somers jewelry—that's fascinating, they like to do that for hours at a time, and we sit on the closet floor and they put all the greens with the greens and the pinks with the pinks."

"You sit on the closet floor?" I jumped in, remembering the times she spent in a closet, trying to stay clear of her drunken father.

"I'm very involved in my closet. It's my own private space and I'm constantly organizing and cleaning out, and 'making nice.' I also hid in the closet most of my childhood so I wonder if it's that. I don't know. But my jewelry box is in the closet and the girls know it's all my Home Shopping jewelry. They like to come in and we close the door and we sit on the floor. It's not large. They're two little people and we're cramped in there and we lay out all the bracelets and the rings and the necklaces and they make color combinations or they match up the colors. They're so awed by it."

So the talented and successful Suzanne Somers is still retreating to her confined spaces from time to time, but now she's been joined by her grandkids, who are happy to play right alongside, safe and secure.

CHAPTER 45

PLAYING BALL WITH ACTOR ED HARRIS

> "When we were kids there was this network of guys calling each other to get together for a baseball game, a football game—or it would be organized before we left school on Friday, and we'd meet Saturday morning at 10:00 and we'd play all day."

That's four-time Academy Award®-nominated actor Ed Harris reminiscing about his fond memories of childhood. Ed's love for sports started when he was just five and his family moved to a neighborhood in Tenafly, New Jersey. He was befriended by a neighborhood kid, Tommy Shadek, and his two brothers. They were very athletic and were into playing all kinds of games.

"During the baseball season my friends and I would play baseball all the time; then in football season we'd play tackle football all the time. We'd play in the snow, we'd play in the house, and we'd play 'knee football.' It was totally fun. You'd play on your knees in the hallway and you'd have three guys on a team. I remember that's all we did. I mean, I was a good student but we just played all the time."

This was fine with his dad who had missed out on a lot of sports when he was a kid. "My Dad was always a sports lover but he had a sister born before him who had died at two weeks, and his mother, in this little town in Oklahoma, was very protective of him and wouldn't let him play organized sports at all—after school basketball or anything. So he totally encouraged my brothers and me to play sports because he hadn't."

Ed recalls that his main baseball thrill was playing catcher and, from the time he was eight years old, that was his position. He even got an inquiry letter from the major league Philadelphia Phillies when he was in high school but, in his own words, "I wasn't that good and I couldn't hit worth a damn, but I was an awfully good defensive catcher."

He was also a big fan. From his earliest days he avidly read the sports pages to see how his beloved New York Yankees were doing. One of the reasons had to do with the player he most idolized. "Mickey Mantle was so much a hero to me when I was growing up. He was 'The Mick.'"

Years later, once he had become a well-known actor, Ed finally had the chance to meet "The Mick," and yet he was still intimidated by the sight of his childhood hero. He had just entered the Regency Hotel in New York and spotted Mantle standing in the lobby. Finally a mutual acquaintance introduced them and Mantle spoke first to the awed Ed Harris. "I don't like you! I'm a big Patsy Cline fan and you weren't nice to her!"

Mantle was obviously joking; referring to the Charlie Dick character Ed had played in the film biography of Patsy Cline's life. However, before the conversation ended, Ed got up enough courage to ask for a signed photo, not so much for himself but for his childhood friend Peter Balakian, who was also a huge fan.

Ed has vivid memories of his childhood summers, when the Harris family would pack up and head to Oklahoma to visit the grandparents. There he was first introduced to table games. "My granddad was a big dominos player and I remember fondly watching him shuffle the dominos because he had these big, long hands and he caressed the ivory. It was kind of beautiful."

On his visits the participants also got very competitive playing "Canasta" and "Scrabble," and that's when Ed first realized that he hated to lose. "I'm not bad now but when I was a kid I was awful. I was an awful loser. It was not pleasant. My parents would just say, 'Ed, it's not that important. What's wrong with you?' I don't remember too many lectures because it was a lost cause."

As a teenager his interest in football took center stage. His high school freshman team went undefeated and, after three years of varsity football, with him as team captain in his senior year, he was offered a scholarship to play for Columbia University. His first year of college ball went well but then a crisis occurred. "I was working out for football after my freshman year and I just couldn't get into it. I wasn't excited about it anymore, which was shocking to me but I had to face it. It had ceased to be fun on some level."

And fun has always been the most important thing to him in his play activities. He recalls an exciting make-believe game he enjoyed, probably a precursor to his later career choice. It was with his younger brother where he, as Davey Crockett, would wrestle a knife away from an attacking Indian.

Then there were the many fishing trips with his dad. They'd go fishing for bass and, though he was never successful at catching a really big fish, it didn't matter because he was out in nature and having a good time. One memory still haunts him.

"It was getting dark and my Dad hooked something that he swore was this huge bass but we never got it in. I think the line broke. I've always wanted to write some story about going back there 30 years later with my father and this lake's probably all polluted and there's this gigantic bass that my Dad catches!"

As for the sports activities that consumed him as a child, he's still into them whenever he can find the time. But age is catching up a bit. "My two brothers and my Dad and I had an annual Christmas touch football game that we played until five or six years ago but my Dad got a little too old. Still we usually try to have a catch if I go back home but we don't do much running around."

It is clear that Ed's play instinct is still very much alive. "I love games. It's very relaxing to play anything. It demands your focus and your attention and I like doing things *well*, and it's fun."

And does the whole family get involved? "Well my wife (actress Amy Madigan) is not a game player. When my folks come to visit I'll try to get her into a game but she resists. My daughter likes games though. She likes playing cards, she likes playing Scrabble." And giggling Ed adds: "I think it's genetic."

CHAPTER 46

PERRY KING'S FAVORITE PLAYMATE

"There are no days in life so memorable as those which vibrated to some stroke of the imagination."
—Ralph Waldo Emerson, American Writer (1803-1882)

Successful film and television actor Perry King (*Riptide, Melrose Place*) remembers having a unique childhood friend named "Scartrout." It was a life-size puppet that his mother had stitched and stuffed so that Perry and his older brother would have a surrogate focus for their emotions and imagination. Scartrout looked like a cowboy villain from 1950s movies. He had a scar on his face and a pencil-thin mustache. Actually Perry still has the fourth reincarnation of him in his home. The other three got beat up so badly that they fell apart. This one wears some of Perry's boyhood clothes—a corduroy shirt and a pair of jeans.

As Perry remembers it, "I didn't have any friends who played the games I played, or could get involved in them on the level that I needed to get involved in. I'd play scenes and Scartrout and I would be cowboys and we'd be gambling and he'd cheat and try to shoot me and I'd draw my gun and I would shoot him. Or it would be a World War II movie where I was the American, the good guy, and he'd be a Nazi and he'd always lose.

"So it would be either with Scartrout and these imaginary scene-like games, or I'd play with toy soldiers. I had a couple of different armies. I had a World War II American army and some Germans and I had a Napoleonic army that was very hard to put together because nobody sold such a thing, so I had to create it by using a lot of Mexican soldiers from an Alamo set.

"There wasn't any toy store so you had to find them where you could. I wanted cannons for my army so badly and I found them at this grocery store. They were selling little toy rubber cannons. I bought one with the one or two dollars I had to my name and I brought it home and it had a little imperfection in it. I tried to cut this imperfection out with a razor blade. It looked worse so I tried to cut that, and make it look better.

"Pretty soon before I knew it, I cut the cannon into pieces, destroyed it, so I went back to the grocery store and spent my last remaining dollar on another cannon, brought it home and destroyed that one too the same way. So then I went back to the grocery store and had no money; so I stole another cannon and destroyed that one. And then I went back to the grocery store and they were out of cannons. It was a real lesson for me that I am prisoner like a lot of people of a desire for things to be perfect. Obviously you have to learn to accept imperfection in your life.

"The most fun I ever had with these armies was when I set them up in the backyard with trenches or battle scenes. But also there was this big table someone had set up for me in the attic of this barn behind our house and I put a lot of earth on this table so I could set up a real diorama, and could play with it at face level. I'd set up various scenes like Waterloo with the British cavalry attacking.

"My parents, in an effort to help me figure out a career, looked at my love of armies and soldiers, assumed I wanted to be a soldier, and took me to see West Point when I was about 12 years old. We looked at all the cadets marching around and I immediately realized two things—one, I loved the uniforms and two, I did not want to go to West Point or be part of the army. I just loved the fantasy!"

Perry ultimately discovered that all this play-acting and fantasy as a child was preparing him to be the fine artist he has become. "I try to bring the same kind of simple, pure, unquestioning commitment to the game I was playing as a kid to the way I act today. I'm convinced that's the way you do it best and most actors agree."

He also remembers his father's advice to him. "Do something with your life that you'd do for free because you love it so much, and then figure out how to make a living at it." So when he was 15 and spending the summer on Nantucket Island in Massachusetts he noticed this community theatre and found out they allowed apprentices to work there. After getting a chance to be onstage and enjoying the thrill of it, he figured out he wanted to make it his career.

A few years ago he finally got to be in a cowboy movie, *The Cowboy and the Showgirl*, something he had waited for his entire life. He believes it's some of the best work he's ever done because he had been thinking and preparing for the part for more than 40 years—ever since he first started having those shoot-em-out saloon card games with Scartrout in the attic of his house when he was just eight years old.

And how does Perry play as an adult? "One of the purposes of my toys these days is to balance what I do as a professional. What I do as an actor is very uncertain, very imprecise. There is no right or wrong, there's nothing black or white about it. So what I like to do has a measurable result in a play sense. I love to race cars. You come in first, second, third, crash—it's absolutely undeniable what happens in a race car. Also I love to fix machines. Well you either fix them or you don't. It's unlike what I do professionally and it's very satisfying. But it all has to do with movement and transportation. I love motorcycles; I love cars, horses, bicycles. Some of that is play-acting fantasy. I always wanted to be a race car driver. I think that racing is powerful and dramatic. So I'm fantasizing as I play at race car driving but it's also surprising how much racing is like acting. You can't think about anything but *right now* and it's satisfying. It's like play and it's like acting."

Perhaps his favorite adult toys are his motorcycles. He now owns 19 of them, and he can trace them directly back to his childhood. "It had a lot to do with the games I played as a kid. In those World War II movies you'd always see these exotic motorcycles with the sidecar. They always fascinated me."

PART EIGHT

ENJOYING THE FUN LIFE

CHAPTER 47

EVERYDAY PLEASURES

"Find ecstasy in life; the mere sense of living is joy enough."
—*Emily Dickinson, American Poet (1830-1886)*

Harley Potter was 103 years old and lived in Winston-Salem, North Carolina when I read about him in a newspaper a few years ago. He had just won the 100-and-over division at the U.S. Senior Sports Classic Golf Tournament. He also happened to be the *only* contestant! Potter's daughter told *Inside Sports* magazine her father's secret to longevity. "He has always said he doesn't worry about yesterday because it's gone or about tomorrow because it's not here."

These are wise words. So much of our anxiety and stress concern being caught up in the past and fretting over something we did, or didn't do, or should have done. Other times we project things into the future and worry about what might happen and how we would cope with it if it was really bad. All the while we're robbing ourselves of the moment. Harley Potter stayed in his zone and just decided to go out and play golf that day. I believe that even if he had had competition and lost he would have had a great time anyway.

Rabbi Steve Leder, a spiritual leader at the Wilshire Boulevard Temple, one of the largest Jewish congregations in Los Angeles, once introduced me at a program for his men's group in a unique way. He cited the Talmud, the collection of writings that constitute the Jewish civil and religious law, and informed the audience that when people die and are called to account on the Day of Judgment, what is measured are all the pleasures one could have enjoyed on

Earth and didn't. It was his way of endorsing the philosophy that fun and play are pleasures to be embraced without guilt.

When you watch the Olympic Games on television be aware that Baron Pierre De Coubertin, the driving force behind the re-establishment of the Games in 1896, said: "The important thing in the Olympic Games is not to win but to take part. The important thing in life is not the triumph but the struggle. The essential thing is not to have conquered but to have fought well."

Dorothy Bird Nyswander died in 1998 at the age of 104. Known as the mother of health education, she helped establish the School of Public Health at the University of California, Berkeley in 1946. Later on she worked for the World Health Organization setting up public health education programs in 12 nations. Her revolutionary approach to health education involved putting people in charge of identifying their own public health problems and solving them. Asked the secret to long life she advised: "Have as much fun as you can and love people."

Ruth Riley Vaughn of Glendora once wrote this letter to the *Los Angeles Times*:

> "I tune my radio to the station featuring the Big Band sound and all the music of the 30s, 40s and 50s. I pour a cup of coffee, listen and let my mind wander. For a little while I'm young, it's Saturday night and I'm all dressed up waiting for my date. Each song brings back a memory of a time, a place, and my "date," who later became my husband. He's gone now, but the music brings him back and miraculously I am no longer alone. The dark corners disappear with the music and the memories."

Angier Biddle Duke, the Chief of Protocol in the Kennedy and

Johnson administrations, died at the age of 79. He was hit by a car and killed while "in-line skating." What a way to go!

In a story in *Reader's Digest*, W.F. Bettwy of Vienna, Virginia reported that on every flight he made out of Washington, D.C. he noticed that his fellow pilot always looked down intently on a certain valley in the Appalachians.

"What's so interesting about that spot?" he asked him one day.

"See that stream? Well when I was a kid, I used to sit down there on a log, fishing. Every time an airplane flew over, I would look up and wish I were flying. Now I look down and wish I were fishing."

CHAPTER 48

IT'S TIME FOR A LITTLE "INTERNAL JOGGING"

"A good laugh is sunshine in the house."
—William Thackeray, English Novelist (1811-1863)

Norman Cousins, as I've reported, stimulated himself back to health from a critical illness by watching comedy videos. In his book, *Anatomy of an Illness,* he discussed the significance of laughter, calling it "internal jogging." His research showed that a robust laugh gives the muscle of the face, shoulders, diaphragm, and abdomen a good workout, and sometimes even the arms and legs. Heart rate and blood pressure temporarily rise, breathing becomes faster and deeper, and oxygen surges throughout the bloodstream. The muscles go limp and blood pressure may fall, leaving one in a mellow euphoria. A good laugh can burn up as many calories per hour as brisk walking. Furthermore, he wrote:

> "What was significant about the laughter also was not just the fact that it provides internal exercise for a person, a form of jogging for the innards, but that it creates a mood in which the other positive emotions can be put to work, too."

Some researchers speculate that laughter triggers the release of endorphins—the brain opiates. That may be why Cousins claimed that ten minutes of belly laughter had an anesthetic effect and would give him at least two hours of pain-free sleep.

A growing number of American hospitals, nursing homes and

recuperation centers now bring in clowns, provide "humor carts" to distribute funny books and videos, or send patients to "humor rooms" for daily doses of jokes and laughter.

It has been found that laughing can reduce stress by lowering levels of cortisol, a stress hormone that can weaken the immune system. Lee Berk and Stanley Tan of Loma Linda University in California did an experiment in which they had a group of healthy men watch a 60-minute humorous video. In their measurements they found significant increases of interferon-gamma, a hormone that fights viruses and regulates cell growth, and that those levels remained higher than normal 12 hours later.

Another study showed that laughter can also stimulate mental functions, such as alertness and memory, perhaps by raising levels of adrenaline and other chemicals that prepare the body for action. They noted a wave of electricity sweeping through the entire brain half a second after the punch line of a joke.

So I implore you—please find ways to laugh. Read the funny papers, seek out humorous films, go to comedy clubs, have your friends tell you jokes, go to the parks and watch how kids run around and have the best time. Make it your business to increase those laughs. It will make you feel a lot better.

CHAPTER 49

THE NEW TECHNOLOGY— A GAME YOU CAN MASTER

> "Be fully in the moment, open yourself to the powerful energies dancing around you."
> —Ernest Hemingway, American Novelist (1899-1961)

A few years back the *Leader's Digest*, an in-house publication of the Internal Revenue Service, interviewed me for an article they were preparing, "The Blurring Line Between Work And Home: New Technology—Who's In Charge?" Their concern was that the new technology was beginning to blur the lines between a person's job and their family and leisure life.

Discussing those ever-present cell phones, the author noted that one's "social life and work may collide at any moment." Although "it's possible to drive the kids to soccer practice and talk to a business associate on the phone—is it wise?" she wondered. My response to her, as reported in the magazine, was that it not only presented the physical danger of driving while talking (accidents caused by cell phone users are mounting), but also that it set an unhealthy example for our kids.

In my words: "Children learn by observation. They may not have the words for it but they understand that Daddy or Mommy is a workaholic. They don't like it, but that's how we pick up those habits that we learn, by observing how our parents did it."

The article also reported how vacations were being infiltrated by the business office back at home. They reminded the reader of the television commercial in which a man is sitting on a tropical beach in a lounge chair. Suddenly his cell phone rings with an urgent call from his boss. He reaches for his laptop and sends the boss the report he was looking for. All the while, you hear a child's voice in the background. She calls impatiently for her father who finally says, "Coming sweetheart," as he lays aside his laptop.

With the glut of pagers, cell phones, e-mail, voice mail, and laptops, employees are now supposed to be ready to work at any time from any place. Is this the way it should be? I say "no," believing we're becoming a society of beeper junkies and cell phone compulsives.

CareerBuilder, a job search and recruitment firm, conducted a survey of more than 1,300 randomly selected workers. More than half of those polled said they planned to stay in touch with work while on vacation, up from 40 percent the year before.

A second survey of 645 business executives, conducted by the American Management Association, found that one-quarter of the executives planned to be in daily contact with the office while on vacation, and more than 60 percent planned to check in at least once a week.

What's the trade-off when your connection to work is not just 24/7, but 365 days a year? "You're not going to gain all the benefit you could from time away from the office," says Arthur Brief, an organizational psychologist and professor at the Tulane University School of Business. Among the benefits you may miss out on, he says, are relief from stress and anxiety. Instead of feeling relaxed and rejuvenated, you could return home feeling pretty much like you did when you left.

Brooks Gump, an assistant professor of psychology at the State University of New York in Oswego, has researched the health benefits of vacationing and has some important statistics. Gump's study, part of a larger trial, included more than 12,000 middle-age men who were at high risk for heart disease. He found that the more often these men took annual vacations, the less likely they were to die from heart disease (this study was done over a nine-year period). Gump thinks that going on vacation may have given these men a chance to let down their guard. But when you pack a cell phone with your sunscreen, you bring along the threat that someone from work could call with a crisis.

Despite the drawbacks, taking work along on vacation is a

new fact of life for many people. Some are required to check in with their bosses, while others choose to do so rather than risk having a project grind to a halt in their absence. Still others simply want reassurance that their jobs will still be waiting when they return. Given this reality, how can you minimize the downside? Leemor Amado, a practice consultant for the American Medical Association, offers these tips:

- Set limits on work time. Pick a period during the day, say between 9 a.m. and 10 a.m., when you will check e-mail and make calls. Then confine work activities to those times, and keep the rest of the day free for rest and relaxation.

- Let people at the office know what to expect. "Tell Betty back at XYZ Corporation that you're going to check in once a day, or twice a week, or whatever," says Amado. "Then stick to it—nothing less, and nothing more."

- Clue in your family and friends, too. Warn those who will be sharing your vacation that you need to work for a limited period every day or so, but promise not to let this take over the whole trip. Then keep your promise.

We can see the new technology as a helpful tool, but not something we should turn to constantly and compulsively. I was particularly horrified when I observed the "ultimate cell phone user" recently. I had just finished seeing a film at a local movie house and headed for the theatre bathroom before going to dinner with a friend. There, at one of the urinals, stood a guy "multi-tasking." He had his cell phone in one hand and...."

A *USA TODAY* report suggests that "the assault of technology, from e-mail to cell phones, is causing a backlash against electronic overkill, the Internet and the barrage of the digital lifestyle." In the year 2000, 29 million U.S. adults stopped using the Net and more than one-third of U.S. consumers surveyed by Harris Online said they suffer from "digital distress," or nervousness and anxiety, in shopping for high-tech goods. About 60% of those who communicated with the interviewers said they have given up trying to keep pace with technology.

According to career experts and social scientists, many people are escaping the high-tech rat race to seek more time with their families, finding solace in nature or getting back to doing things that make them happy such as gardening, biking, and other playful pursuits. I implore you to do the same.

CHAPTER 50

YES, PLAYMATES, THERE "IS" A SANTA CLAUS!

"Christmas isn't a season. It's a feeling."
—Edna Ferber, American Novelist (1885-1968)

Many people in the world don't look forward to Christmas or the other festive holidays that occur in December. Unlike most of us they have trouble experiencing the joys of the season. Perhaps they believe the holidays have become too commercial. Or maybe they have bad memories of Christmases past. Or it might be the customs associated with the holidays. There has always been concern about the Santa Claus myth and how children are made to believe that there's a rotund man riding around in a sled pulled by nine reindeer, climbing down chimneys to bring toys to every child in the world on Christmas Eve.

There's even a famous article, written more than 100 years ago that deals with the subject. In 1897 an eight-year-old named Virginia O'Hanlon wrote a letter to the now defunct *New York Sun* newspaper concerned about some information she had been told. Here is that letter:

> "Dear Editor: I am 8 years old. Some of my
> little friends say there is no Santa Claus.
> Papa says, 'If you see it in the New York Sun,
> it's so.' Please tell me the truth. Is there
> a Santa Claus?"—Virginia O'Hanlon

In response Francis P. Church, the editor of the paper wrote this letter back. I share it with you, in its entirety, because it has a lot to say about joy, about childhood, and about the many wonders of the lives we lead.

> "Dear Virginia: Your friends are wrong. They have been affected by the skepticism of a skeptical age. They do not believe except what they can see. They think that nothing can be which is not comprehensible by their little minds. All minds, Virginia, whether they be men's or children's, are little.
>
> In this great universe of ours, man is a mere insect, an ant, in his intellect, as compared with the boundless world around him, as measured by the intelligence capable of grasping the whole truth and knowledge.
>
> Yes, Virginia, there is a Santa Claus. He exists as certainly as love and generosity and devotion exist, and you know that they abound and give to your life its highest beauty and joy. Alas! How dreary would be the world if there were no Santa Claus. It would be as dreary as if there were no Virginias.
>
> There would be no childlike faith then, no poetry, no romance to make tolerable this existence. We should have no enjoyment, except in sense and sight. The eternal light with which childhood fills the world would be extinguished.

Not believe in Santa Claus! You might as well not believe in fairies! You might get your papa to hire men to watch in all the chimneys on Christmas Eve to catch Santa Claus coming down, but what would that prove? Nobody sees Santa Claus, but there is no sign that there is no Santa Claus.

The most real things in the world are those that neither children nor men can see. Did you ever see fairies dancing on the lawn? Of course not, but that's no proof that they are not there. Nobody can conceive or imagine all the wonders that are unseen and unseeable in the world. You tear apart the baby's rattle to see what makes the noise inside, but there is a veil covering the unseen world which not the strongest man nor even the unified strength of all the strongest men that ever lived could tear apart. Only faith, fancy, poetry, love, romance can push aside that curtain and view and picture the supernatural beauty and glory beyond. Is it all real? Ah, Virginia, in all this world there is nothing else real and abiding.

No Santa Claus! Thank God he lives, and he lives forever. A thousand years from now, Virginia, nay 10 times 10,000 years from now, he will continue to make glad the heart of childhood."

CHAPTER 51

DR. PLAY'S "HEALTHFUL HINTS"

"Everything has been said before, but since nobody listens we have to keep going back and beginning all over again."
—*Andre Gide, French Critic and Novelist (1869-1951)*

I willingly hand out prescriptions for the maintenance of good health, but they don't involve drugs or antibiotics of any kind. Rather I believe we all need to listen to that little voice inside that talks to us all the time and to find ways to make our day more playful. The following is a reminder of a number of things that you can do whenever you're stressed or "down," or just trying to find a way to bring more joy into your life. Keep this list in a handy place. Hey, LET'S PLAY AGAIN.

PLAY WITH A FRIEND!
- Know just which buddy to call when you're about to snap or are particularly stressed. Ask them to say something funny or soothing or to tell you an amusing story.
- Find a "playmate" at your work site that you can visit whenever you can't cope with the craziness that is swirling around you.
- Make a date with your mate to play miniature golf, or spend time carousing the mall hand-in-hand, or go bowling together. Perhaps best of all, have an evening "playing in bed"—and that can mean "Scrabble" or whatever your mind and bodies can create.

PLAY WITH YOURSELF!
- Get out one or two of the toys that you've stocked in your office for just this moment of tension, and play with them.
- Read a few pages of that terrific book you just started. It will instantly take you away from the present unrest.
- Take a mini-vacation at your desk. Close your eyes and transport yourself to another locale—a warm, sandy beach; an incredible ski run; the vacation you took last year; the vacation you want to take next year; or go back into your childhood and see yourself having a wonderful experience of "recess."
- Treat yourself to a walk and discover something new and fun about your surroundings.
- Find a secret place to "go skipping." See if you remain agitated after that!
- Stop and smell the crayons; watch a sunrise or a sunset; listen to your favorite music; hug yourself.

PLAY WITH YOUR FOOD!
- Blow bubbles in your iced tea.
- Take the "fruit break" I talked about in Chapter 31.
- Buy a side of mashed potatoes at lunch and really mash them rather than venting your anger on someone else.
- Seek out a favorite comfort food (chocolate bar, peanut butter, lollipop, apple turnover, licorice) and indulge yourself.

PLAY WITH YOUR JOB!
- See your job as a game.
- Find ways to laugh at what you're doing.
- It's not brain surgery so lighten up about your responsibilities and your instinct perhaps to be a "workaholic."
- Wear outrageous underwear under your business clothes.
- If you're stuck without a solution for a difficult issue, brainstorm a wacky, new method of accomplishing your goal. It may end up being the best way after all.

PLAY WHEREVER YOU ARE!
- Connect with waiters and waitresses, supermarket cashiers and baggers, and sales personnel by seeing if you can make them smile or laugh. If nothing else you might end up getting better service.
- Wave at children on school buses and see how gleefully they'll respond.
- While riding on a crowded elevator in your office building, say something funny out loud like, "Third Floor, Lingerie!"
- When passing through a bridge or tunnel toll booth, pay for the car behind you and see what happens.

Smile and laugh whenever you can!

CHAPTER 52

HAVING FUN ON THE JOURNEY

"Be aware of wonder. Live a balanced life—learn some and think some, and draw and paint and sing and dance and play and work every day some."
—Robert Fulghum, American Author (1937-present)

I always end my seminars with a short motivational passage—an essay or poem written by someone other than me, capturing their "take" on this great journey called life. Though I have many to choose from, and handpick them for specific groups, the three that follow are probably my favorites.

The first piece was written several years ago by Nadine Stair, a senior citizen living in Louisville, Kentucky. On the occasion of her 93rd birthday she decided to write a short essay in which she reflected on her life, and talked about the changes she would make if she had the chance to do it all over again.

IF I HAD MY LIFE TO LIVE OVER
"If I had my life to live over, I would dare to make more mistakes next time. I would relax. I would limber up. I would be 'sillier' than I've been this time. I would take fewer things serious and I would take more chances. I'd take more trips, I'd climb more mountains, and I'd swim more rivers. I would eat more ice cream and less beans.

"I would perhaps have more actual troubles, but I would have fewer imaginary ones. You see I am one of those people who live sensibly and sanely hour after hour, day after day.

"Oh, I've had my moments, but if I had to do it over again,

I'd have more of them. In fact, I'd try to have nothing else—just moments, one after one, instead of living so many years ahead.

"I've been one of those persons who never goes anywhere without a thermometer, a hot water bottle, a raincoat, and a parachute.

"If I had my life to live over, I would start bare-foot earlier in the Spring, and would stay that way later in the Fall. I would go to more dances. I would ride more merry-go-rounds. I would pick more daisies."

One of my favorite clients is Glenda Berman, Employee Services Manager for the City of Beverly Hills. She is an upbeat, extraordinarily competent person, and I enjoy being in her company. At a seminar for one of her departments, I closed with Nadine Stair's essay. Afterwards Glenda told me that she had in her possession a different "If I Had My Life to Live Over" letter that she thought I should see. She said it was from an anonymous source. Liking it very much, I decided to include it at the end of some of my seminars.

Eventually I was surprised to learn that it had been written by Erma Bombeck, one of Johnny Carson's favorite *Tonight Show* guests. Unlike many of Erma's witty writings, it's a more introspective piece, composed when she learned that she had cancer. Here, she talks about a few of her perceived missteps in life and how she would change them. I am often moved to tears when I read this piece, particularly the last two sentences.

IF I HAD MY LIFE TO LIVE OVER #2

"If I had my life to live over, I would talk less and listen more. I would invite friends over to dinner even though the carpet was stained and the sofa was faded.

"I would eat popcorn in the 'good living room' and worry less about the dirt when someone wanted to light a fire in the fireplace.

"I would burn the pink candle sculpted like a rose before it melted in storage.

"I would sit on the lawn with my children and not worry about grass stains.

"I would cry and laugh less while watching television—and do it more while living life.

"I would share more of the responsibilities carried by my spouse.

"I would go to bed when I was sick instead of worrying that the Earth would go into a holding pattern if I missed work for one day.

"I would never buy anything just because it was practical, wouldn't show soil, or was guaranteed to last a lifetime.

"There would be more statements of 'I love you,' more 'I am sorry.'

"But mostly, given another shot at life, I would seize every moment, look at it and really see it and live it and never give it back."

It doesn't matter to me what your true age is, but I do hope you are in good health. I'm not concerned if you have lots of money or have to struggle with every paycheck. I don't care where you were born or where you live now. It's not important to me whether your life is very simple or very complex.

What I care most is that you realize that no matter your circumstances, you always have the capacity and the choice to "feel young." Here is an anonymous little piece that covers it all, and I thank you for reaching this point in my book.

YOU ARE STILL YOUNG

"A child opens his and her arms to each new day,
Eager to experience all that life has to offer.
The beauty in a drop of rain
The vastness of the sky
The sweetness of a loved one's voice.
We watch as he marvels at the metamorphosis of a caterpillar
And we say, "You are still young."
You have not the cares nor the worries of those older
than you.

You have the freedom to explore.
And we envy the child.
Still a child exists within us all, no matter what our age.
When we embrace that joy with all our being
Then we, too, behold the wonders of each new day.
For we are still young."

Now please put the book down, smile at yourself in the mirror, change into some comfortable clothes, give yourself a hug, and go outside and play. When's Recess? Right now—and you have Dr. Play's total permission.

ISBN 1412033462

Printed in Great Britain
by Amazon